GERMAN BUSINESS CORRESPONDENCE COURSE

1034666   X

GERMAN BUSINESS CORRESPONDENCE COURSE

Paul Hartley
B.A., M.Phil., Ph.D., F.I.L.

School of Languages and European Studies
The Polytechnic, Wolverhampton

MACMILLAN MULTILINGUAL BUSINESS SERIES

MACMILLAN

First published 1989

Published by
MACMILLAN EDUCATION LTD
Houndmills, Basingstoke, Hampshire RG21 2XS
and London
Companies and representatives
throughout the world

Typeset by Gecko Limited, Bicester, Oxon

Printed in Hong Kong

British Library Cataloguing in Publication Data
Hartley, Paul
    German business correspondence course –
    (Macmillan multilingual business series)
    1. International business correspondence
    in German — Manuals
    I. Title
    808′.066651031

ISBN 0–333–49434–2

CONTENTS

ABOUT THIS COURSE

The principle on which the *Multilingual Business Correspondence Course* is based is a simple one. Analysis of any significant corpus of business correspondence reveals that a number of relatively unchanging, context-independent linguistic formulae, in conjunction with a number of context-dependent terms and expressions, account for a significant proportion of the content of business letters.

These formulae, terms and expressions can be regarded as the building blocks of written communications between firms. Letter-writing in the foreign language becomes a considerably easier task if students have access to these building blocks and, through regular practice, are able to assimilate them into their active vocabulary.

The *Multilingual Business Handbook*, with which this Course is intended to be used, gives students easy access to some 1800 of these building blocks in each of 5 languages.

The *Multilingual Business Correspondence Course*, of which this German course is a part, provides students with the practice required to assimilate them.

This is not of course to say that a knowledge of fixed formulae, terms and expressions is in itself sufficient to account for the creativity inherent in writing business letters in a foreign language, merely that it can provide a useful starting point. The terms and expressions which are contained in the *Multilingual Business Handbook* and used in this Course are no substitute for competence in the foreign language, but they can both help students develop that competence and provide accomplished linguists with access to the business language with which they may be unfamiliar.

INTRODUCTION

This course is intended for Intermediate or Advanced level students of foreign languages for business purposes. In designing the Course two major considerations have been borne in mind: that it should be a teaching course and that it should be compatible with modern approaches to language teaching.

A Teaching Course

Regrettably, students often come to perceive letter-writing in the foreign language as an arduous dictionary-based task reminiscent of unseen prose translation. This Course sets out to counter that perception by creating a graded, supportive and realistic learning environment which helps students acquire the translation and composition skills required to deal with business correspondence. This is achieved in the following way:

- Letters are graded in order of increasing linguistic and situational difficulty. Students learn how to compose complex business letters by first dealing with simpler ones.
- The teaching/learning process is supported at every stage by the *Multilingual Business Handbook*. Most of the letters are accompanied by a translation aid in the form of a 'skeleton' of key letters and numbers (A1, B7, R77 etc.) which act as pointers to terms and expressions contained in the *Multilingual Business Handbook*. The provision of 'skeletons' dispenses with the need for lengthy dictionary searches and permits students to deal with complex correspondence relatively quickly.
- Every section contains two scenarios of three letters each. These letters simulate a continuing exchange about a specific issue, for example a disputed insurance claim or damage to goods in transit. The realism implicit in this simulation means that in the classroom, as in real business practice, one can frequently derive key terms, expressions and structures from previous exchanges within the same context, and use them to aid the production of the new letter. This Course is designed to model the association of incoming with outgoing correspondence and to do so in exchanges of increasing linguistic and situational difficulty.

Modern Approaches to Language Teaching

Modern approaches to teaching languages for business purposes tend to assess student learning by means of integrated exercises or assignments. These consist of simulations of business activities involving case studies, role playing and the deployment of a range of listening, speaking, reading and writing skills to accomplish a set of realistic tasks. The translating and writing of business letters normally feature quite prominently in the assignment-based approach, not only because of the realism inherent in such tasks but also because they act as an appropriate vehicle for practising writing in the foreign language. This Course aims precisely to provide, within the context of the assignment-based approach, the regularity of practice and the gradual development of skills necessary for successful letter writing in the foreign language.

Modern approaches to learning business languages also tend to stress the importance of autonomous learning, information retrieval and the use of appropriate materials and technologies to support these activities. This course is uniquely placed in this respect, since it is intended to be used with the *Multilingual Business Handbook*.

This is a definitive guide to commercial letter writing in English, French, German, Spanish and Italian and is currently published in Britain, France, Germany, Italy, Holland, Spain and the United States. It contains approximately 1800 expressions and phrases in each language, divided into sections such as Enquiries and Offers, Orders, etc. Within each section, every expression has a key letter and number (A36, B39 etc.) which corresponds exactly to the appropriate expression in each of the other languages.

Most of the letters in the *Multilingual Business Correspondence Course* are accompanied by a 'skeleton' of the form (A1, A7, B26, C90 etc.) which enables the student to retrieve from the Handbook key phrases which will be of help in the translation of the associated letter.

An Integrated Package

In combination with the *Multilingual Business Handbook* and the *LinguaWrite Computer Database*, the *Multilingual Business Correspondence Course* provides an integrated and pedagogically sound learning package which is compatible with modern language teaching practice. It can be used on a stand-alone basis or as a complement to the assignment-based approach to enable students to learn about business correspondence by translating and writing letters of increasing complexity. Furthermore the database provides students with the opportunity of using information technology as an integral part of the learning process, and can be used with the computer's word-processing facility to enable letters of business quality to be produced.

HOW TO USE THIS COURSE

The Course Structure

The course is divided into 15 sections, each of which is based on one or more sections of the *Multilingual Business Handbook*. The sections are further divided into two sub-sections, A and B, with three letters in each. Each letter is identified according to the sub-section and section to which it belongs. For example, Section 1 of the course contains letters 1A1, 1A2, 1A3, 1B1, 1B2 and 1B3. Section 2 contains letters 2A1, 2A2, 2A3, 2B1, 2B2 and 2B3, etc.

Different Paths through the Course

Those letters whose identifier contains the letter 'A' are primarily intended for use by students who have already completed a course of study in German, and who are continuing with the language in preparation for A/S level or the intermediate awards of bodies such as BTEC, RSA, Institute of Linguists or LCCI. Those letters whose identifier contains the character 'B' are primarily intended for use by higher diploma or degree level students of German for business purposes, including those preparing for higher level RSA or Institute of Linguists Examinations. The Course thus provides for different start-levels according to the students' prior experience of the language.

Teachers wishing to provide a course aimed primarily at post-GCSE (or equivalent) students can work on the simpler sub-section A of each section, whilst post-'A' Level (or equivalent) students can therefore work on the corresponding but more complex sub-section B. Conversely teachers may decide to ignore this distinction and simply work through the Course section by section, selecting letters from both sub-sections as they see fit.

Different paths can thus be followed through the Course according to student needs.

Section Layout

Each section of the Course deals with a different type of letter and is divided into two sub-sections comprising three letters each. The three letters are associated by situation and context, simulating ongoing correspondence between foreign and British companies. Letter 1 of each sub-section is written in the foreign language for translation into the student's mother tongue. A 'skeleton' of key letters and numbers taken from the *Multilingual Business Handbook* points the student towards the key phrases contained in the letter and acts as a translation aid. Each sub-section has been devised so that many of the terms and expressions learned by the student in the course of translating letter 1 into his/her mother tongue can subsequently be used to translate letter 2 into the target language. Again a 'skeleton' is provided for this translation task. Letter 3 then provides the opportunity for further practice, continuing the exchange commenced by letters 1 and 2 but allowing the student freer expression, not only because of its guided composition format, but also because it is not accompanied by a 'skeleton' derived from the *Handbook*. Typically, then, the teacher might work with students on letters 1 and 2 in class and set the associated letter 3 as a homework exercise.

Progress through the Sections

The letters contained in the sections increase in complexity as students progress through the Course. This increase in complexity manifests itself in a number of ways. Firstly, the situations dealt with in the sections become progressively more elaborate, with a concomitant increase in letter length.

Secondly, the language structures and terminology used increase in difficulty and specificity, and the role of tone is developed. Thirdly, the proportion of a given letter accounted for by the terms and expressions whose key letters and numbers are found in the associated skeleton diminishes as the Course proceeds. This is particularly true of the later letters in the foreign language, which are designed to expose students to a variety of terms, expressions and language structures not contained in the *Multilingual Business Handbook*. These are then reworked in the reply, the composition of which is aided by the usual skeleton of key letters and numbers, which point students to helpful terms and expressions in the *Multilingual Business Handbook*. Here again, in the later sections students will be expected to modify these terms and expressions to suit specific situations of use. The need to effect tense shifts, change syntax and substitute vocabulary means that students gradually come to use the building blocks as a springboard for creative writing in the foreign language.

Letter Layout

Letter layout is a moot point. Various sets of 'rules' have been suggested, but in reality the practices adopted by firms often defy these supposed conventions. The various letter layouts used in this Course reflect current business practice and are intended to cover the most important aspects of format in a clear a manner as possible. They should not, however, be regarded as prescriptive and students will, in any case, quickly discover the particular practices of their employer upon starting work or commencing a training period.

Students preparing for public examinations in which letter layout is a component should of course follow the rules for layout prescribed by the Examination Board in question.

SUMMARY OF COURSE AIMS

The *Multilingual Business Correspondence Course* aims to provide:

1. A structured teaching/learning package as opposed to a corpus of business correspondence.
2. Materials which can be equally well used on a stand-alone basis or as part of an assignment-based course.
3. Maximum opportunity for autonomous learning on the part of the student, through its integration with the *Multilingual Business Handbook*.
4. The opportunity for students to use information technology as a regular part of their learning activities, through its integration with the *LinguaWrite Computer Database*.
5. Different paths through the course for students of different language levels.
6. A realistic learning environment in which business letters are associated by function and context in a genuinely communicative manner.
7. A pedagogically sound learning environment in which letter reception precedes letter production.
8. An enjoyable learning experience for students, by focusing on what they can do as opposed to what they cannot.

SECTION 1: ENQUIRIES AND OFFERS

This section is based on terms and expressions contained in Section B of the *MULTILINGUAL BUSINESS HANDBOOK*.

BÜROTIK AG — Lindenallee 45 — 8000 München 2

Telefon: 089 24 36 72
Telex: 521 62 28

Chambers and Wright
32-39 Bloomfield Square

Birmingham B34 6NJ

England

Ihr Zeichen	Ihre Nachricht vom	Unser Zeichen	München
		HO/DK	14.07.19..

Betreff
Anfrage

Sehr geehrte Herren,

von Geschäftsfreunden haben wir erfahren, daß Sie Schreibartikel herstellen. Wir sind Eigentümer von einem großen Versandhaus mit Sitz in München, und wir haben es vor, unser Sortiment zu erweitern.

Wir wären Ihnen dankbar, wenn Sie uns Ihre neueste Broschüre mit Preisliste schicken könnten. Wir interessieren uns besonders für Kugelschreiber und Füllhalter. Wenn wir eine Probebestellung erteilen, und die Preise und Qualität der Waren uns zusagen, ist es möglich, daß wir in größeren Mengen bestellen.

Wir möchten aber darauf hinweisen, daß wir die Waren vor Ende Oktober brauchen. Wegen großer Nachfrage von unseren Kunden geht unser Lagerbestand vor der Weihnachtszeit schnell zu Ende.

Wir hoffen auf baldige Antwort und verbleiben

mit freundlichen Grüßen

H. Ortmeier
Leiter

(*Multilingual Business Handbook skeleton:* B1, B3, I1, B52, B12/13, A45, B135, B31, B56, B17, A123)

Chambers and Wright
Bloomfield Square
Birmingham
England

Tel: 021 385 3657
Telex: CWRIGHT 284594

28 July 19..

Your Reference: HO/DK
Our Reference: SG/ND

Bürotik AG
Lindenallee 45
8000 München 2
West Germany

Dear Sirs

Thank you for your letter of 14 July 19.. We are pleased to enclose our latest catalogues and price list, which we are sure you will find of interest.

We should point out that the prices quoted are without discount. For first orders we can grant a discount of 3% on the catalogue prices, and for subsequent orders a discount of 5%. Obviously, packing is included in our prices, which are quoted c.i.f. Our representative, Mr Charles Wheeler, will ring you next week to give you further details of our new range for Christmas. He is coming to Munich in August, and will visit you then. Please contact us before then if you have any further questions.

Yours faithfully

S. Granger

Sales Manager

(Multilingual Business Handbook skeleton: B78, B128, B80, B129, B103, B110, B64, B59)

Continue the exchange of correspondence by composing a third letter (in German) on the basis of the following notes:

From: H. Ortmeier (Bürotik)

To: S. Granger (Chambers and Wright)

- Thank you for the catalogues and pricelist

- From our present supplier we receive a discount of 6% for large orders

- Can you offer the same discount?

- We shall shortly place a trial order for a number of pens – you should receive this within two weeks

- We shall be pleased to meet your representative in Munich in August.

KÜCHEN HEINO GmbH — Schützenstraße 15 — 7000 Stuttgart 4

Telefon: 0711 24 39 54
Telex: 722519

Colourway Tiles and Ceramics
Unit 23
Harding Trading Estate

Dover

England

Ihr Zeichen	Ihre Nachricht vom	Unser Zeichen	Tag
		FB/DS	3.2.19..

Betreff
Anfrage

Sehr geehrte Herren,

wir sind eine mittelgroße Firma in Stuttgart, und wir spezialisieren uns auf die Herstellung von Einbauküchen. Wir haben über Ihre Firma in den Handelszeitungen gelesen und Ihren Katalog von Geschäftsfreunden erhalten. Wegen Schwierigkeiten mit unserem jetzigen Lieferanten geht unser Lagerbestand an Fliesen in verschiedenen Farben schnell zu Ende, und wir brauchen dringend die folgenden Artikel:

— Fliesen (blau) Katalognummer B/8276 – 3000 St.

— Fliesen (gelb/grün) Katalognummer B/8298 – 2000 St.

— Fliesen (weiß) Katalognummer B/8428 – 5000 St.

Wie schon gesagt, benötigen wir die Lieferung dringend, weil mehrere Kunden schon seit 3 Wochen warten. Wir wären Ihnen dankbar, wenn Sie uns Ihre Preise (einschließlich der Lieferung an die obengenannte Adresse) telefonisch mitteilen könnten. Wir hoffen, daß Sie für Bestellungen in solchen Mengen einen Rabatt auf Ihre Katalogpreise gewähren können.

Wenn Sie die Waren vor Ende März liefern können, und wenn die Qualität unseren Erwartungen entspricht, werden wir größere Aufträge erteilen. Wir hoffen auf baldige Antwort und verbleiben

mit freundlichen Grüßen

F. Berger
Leiter

(*Multilingual Business Handbook skeleton*: B2, B14, B17, D6, B86, B80, B123)

1B2

Colourway Tiles
Harding Trading Estate
Dover
England

Tel: 0304 539828
Fax: 0304 200 284

Your Reference: FB/DS
Our Reference: DL/SC   12.2.19..

Küchen Heino GmbH
Schützenstraße 15
7000 Stuttgart 4
West Germany

Dear Mr Berger

Thank you for your letter of 3 February enquiring about our products. Further to our telephone conversation of 8 February I can now inform you that we are in a position to supply the following:

2000 blue tiles (B/8276)

1500 yellow/green tiles (B/8298)

3000 white tiles (B/8428)

The above can all be delivered within the next two weeks. The remaining items will be delivered by 20 March. I am pleased to inform you that we can grant you an introductory discount of 7% on our catalogue prices, and this offer is firm subject to acceptance by 20 February. These prices, as I indicated on the telephone, include packing and delivery to your factory. I can assure you that your order will be executed to your complete satisfaction.

I am enclosing with this letter a new catalogue, as we have just expanded our range. We hope you will find this of interest. On this new range of tiles we are offering a special discount of 4% for first orders.

I look forward to receiving confirmation of your order very shortly.

Yours sincerely

D. Lawson (Sales Manager)

(*Multilingual Business Handbook skeleton:* A10, B123, 142, B81, B120, B131, B103, A50, B52, B82, B128)

Continue this exchange of correspondence by composing a third letter (in German) on the basis of the following notes:

From: F. Berger

To: D. Lawson

- Thanks for letter of 12 February.

- We confirm order of the items listed in your letter.

- Delivery **must** be within two weeks, or we shall lose customers.

- You didn't include details of conditions of payment in your letter. Please send details a.s.a.p.

- Your new catalogue very interesting — have passed it to various colleagues.

- There is a trade fair in Hamburg from 20 to 23 July this year, and lots of kitchen equipment firms will be represented. You may well find it useful to attend this.

- We can send you further details of this if you wish.

SECTION 2:   ORDERS

This section is based on terms and expressions contained in Section C of the *MULTILINGUAL BUSINESS HANDBOOK*.

MODEHAUS GÜTEMANN — Laienstraße 54 — FRANKFURT/MAIN

Telefon: 069 28 49 38
Telex:411 298

Harris Suedes and Leathers
29 Littlehampton Place

Coventry CV4 2PG

England

Ihr Zeichen	Ihre Nachricht vom	Unser Zeichen	Tag
CS/ST	7. März	LH/DR	14.3.19..

Betreff
Bestellung auf Handtaschen

Sehr geehrte Herren,

wir danken Ihnen für Ihr Schreiben vom 7. März und für Ihren Katalog. Wir freuen uns,
Ihnen mitzuteilen, daß die Artikel in Ihrem Katalog unseren Bedürfnissen entsprechen, und
anbei finden Sie unsere Bestellung Nummer D/2947 auf 60 Damenhandtaschen (Leder/
schwarz, Katalognummer Z2583).

Die Bestellung basiert auf Ihrem Katalogpreis von £18.50 pro Handtasche. Bitte teilen Sie
uns sofort mit, wenn Sie nicht in der Lage sind, vor Ende März zu liefern, da wir die Taschen
vor Ostern brauchen. Wenn wir mit dieser ersten Sendung zufrieden sind, sind wir bereit,
einen Dauerauftrag aufzugeben.

Ich wäre Ihnen dankbar, wenn Sie diese Bestellung sobald wie möglich bestätigen könnten.

Mit freundlichen Grüßen

L. Haller
Abteilungsleiter

(Multilingual Business Handbook skeleton: C3, C11, C9, C15, C4, C8, C63)

HARRIS SUEDES AND LEATHERS
29 Littlehampton Place
Coventry CV4 2PG

Tel: 0203 422469
Telex: 426498

7.3.19...

Your Reference:
Our Reference: DR/SH

Modehaus Gütemann
Laienstraße 54
6000 Frankfurt am Main
West Germany

Dear Mr Haller

Thank your for your order of 14 March. Unfortunately, at the moment we only have in stock 40 of the handbags you ordered, and these are now ready for despatch.

We can either send you 20 handbags in brown leather (at a price of £22.50) immediately, or we could send you the remaining 20 bags in black leather in two weeks' time. We await your further instructions.

We apologise for this delay and remain

Yours sincerely

D. Richmond

Sales Manager

(*Multilingual Business Handbook skeleton:* A10, B20, C58, C60, F67)

Continue this exchange of correspondence by composing a third letter (in German) on the basis of the following notes.

From: L. Haller (Modehaus Gütemann)

To: D. Richmond (Harris Suedes and Leathers)

- Thanks for letter of 7 March.

- Please send us the 40 black leather bags.

- We do not need the brown leather ones, as we find the price a little high.

- If offer could be reduced by 4 or 5% we may order in future.

- Let us know if you could deliver a further 50 black bags by end of April.

- What discount on your catalogue price could you grant on these?

BELZ ELEKTRONIK
Turiner Straße 27   5000 Köln

Telefon: 0221 35 47 59
Telex: 8883957

Automart
43 Foss Way

Reading

England

Ihr Zeichen	Ihre Nachricht vom	Unser Zeichen	Tag
	19. Juni	HP/DF	2.7.19...

Betreff
Ihre Bestellung Nr. BV45/3987

Sehr geehrte Herren,

wir danken Ihnen für Ihr Schreiben und Ihre Bestellung vom 19. Juni. Leider müssen wir Ihren Auftrag etwas ändern. Sie haben 20 Cassettenrecorder (Modell ZTC 820) bestellt – zum Preis von DM360 das Stück.

Wir stellen dieses Modell nicht mehr her, da es durch ein neues Modell (ZTD 842) ersetzt worden ist. Der Preis ist dementsprechend etwas höher (DM465), aber diese Recorder haben 2 Jahre Garantie.

Wir wissen, daß Sie die Recorder binnen 10 Tagen brauchen, und deshalb sind wir bereit, Ihnen einen Rabatt von 4% auf den Katalogpreis zu gewähren, wenn Sie das neue Modell annehmen. Es ist möglich, daß eine unserer Niederlassungen in der Schweiz noch ein paar Cassettenrecorder Modell ZTC 820 auf Lager hat, und diesbezüglich haben wir schon an sie geschrieben.

Bitte teilen Sie uns sobald wie möglich mit, ob wir die Waren versenden sollten.

Mit freundlichen Grüßen

H. Pschorr
Verkaufsleiter

(*Multilingual Business Handbook skeleton:* C1, C30, B58, B39, B80, C14)

Automart
43 Foss Way
Reading
England

Tel: 0734 364839
Telex: AUTMART 392834

9.7.19...

Your Reference: HP/DF
Our Reference: GB/RG

Herrn
P. Schorr
Belz Elektronik
Turiner Straße 26
5000 Köln
West Germany

Dear Mr Pschorr

Thank you for your letter of 2 July regarding our recent order for 20 cassette recorders. We are sorry to learn that you no longer produce the model we ordered, as we have always had a heavy demand for these from our customers.

We should be grateful if you could possibly supply some of the old model (ZTC 820) from one of your other branches, as you suggested.

We find your price for the new model a little high, certainly higher than that of a similar model from another supplier. If you could reduce your offer by about 7 or 8% we could be prepared to place an order for 40 or 50 of this model.

We see from your catalogue that you also manufacture car radios. It is possible that we shall soon be placing a trial order with you for several of these, and I shall be in contact with you shortly on this matter.

Yours sincerely

G. Burnham

Manager

(*Multilingual Business Handbook skeleton:* A22, B56, C18, C21, C19, C20, A77, B125)

Continue the exchange of correspondence by composing a third letter (in German) on the basis of the following notes.

From: H. Pschorr (Belz Elektronik)

To: G. Burnham (Automart)

- One of our branches in Switzerland can supply 10 of the model required, within a week.

- We therefore have to send you 10 of the new model.

- Have reduced our price by 5% as introductory offer.

- For future orders of more than 40 we can offer 9% discount.

- Please inform a.s.a.p. if you wish to take advantage of this offer.

SECTION 3: DELIVERY, TRANSPORT, CUSTOMS

This section is based on terms and expressions contained in Section D of the *MULTILINGUAL BUSINESS HANDBOOK*.

KREEDE UND HOFFMANN
Spielwarenfabrik

Ottomanallee 72   8500 Nürnberg

Telefon: 0911 42 39 38
Telex: 626497

Playorama
72 Holbrook Circus

Liverpool

England

Ihr Zeichen	Ihre Nachricht vom	Unser Zeichen	Tag
GW/AN	14.8.19...	HH/DT	20.9.19...

Betreff
Ihre Bestellung Nummer 743/BR/72

Sehr geehrte Herren,

wir danken Ihnen für Ihre Bestellung für 150 Kinderwagen (Modell 'Sara'). Sie schreiben, daß Sie diese Lieferung dringend benötigen. Leider müssen wir Ihnen mitteilen, daß es wegen gegenwärtiger Produktionsschwierigkeiten nicht möglich ist, die Waren innerhalb der vereinbarten Frist zu liefern. Unser Lagerbestand an Rädern für dieses Modell geht zu Ende, und wir suchen einen anderen Lieferanten, da unser bisheriger Lieferant nicht mehr in der Lage ist, diese Räder in den gewünschten Mengen zu liefern.

Ein Teil Ihrer Bestellung (70 Kinderwagen) ist jetzt versandbereit, und laut Vereinbarung schicken wir diese Wagen per Bahn und Schiff. Sie sollten sie binnen 2 Tagen erhalten. Wir werden unser möglichstes tun, die übrigen 80 Wagen bis Ende des Monats versandbereit zu haben. Wir bedauern sehr die Unannehmlichkeiten, die wir Ihnen bereitet haben.

Mit freundlichen Grüßen

H. Holzer
Verkaufsleiter

(*Multilingual Business Handbook skeleton:* D6, B17, D39, D48, A84, A89)

Playorama
72 Holbrook Circus
Liverpool

Tel: 051 492436
Telex: PLAY 385637

4.10.19...

Your Reference: HH/DT
Our Reference: GW/LN

Herrn
H. Holzer
Kreede und Hoffmann
Ottomanallee 72
8500 Nürnberg
West Germany

Dear Mr Holzer

Thank you for your letter of 20 September. The seventy prams to which you refer in your letter have now arrived. As you are aware, our original order was for 150 of these items, and the delay in delivery of the remaining 80 has caused us considerable difficulties, as many of our customers have been waiting for some time.

We regret to inform you that, unless we receive the rest of our order within three weeks, we may have to order from another supplier.

Yours sincerely

G. Warner

Assistant Manager

(*Multilingual Business Handbook skeleton:* E2, E3, D7, A31)

Continue the exchange of correspondence by composing a third letter (in German) on the basis of the following notes.

From: Kreede und Hoffmann

To: Playorama

- We have now obtained supply of wheels from another manufacturer.

- The order you placed should be ready within a week.

- The goods will be sent by express delivery.

- Apologies for inconvenience.

- We enclose our latest catalogues (to cover Christmas period).

- Hope for further orders.

GEBR. HALLER GmbH
Sesamstraße 87 8400 Regensburg

Ternby Porcelain plc
55-61 Denby Road

Telefon: 0941 42 34 96
Telex: 652856

Stoke on Trent

England

Ihr Zeichen	Ihre Nachricht vom	Unser Zeichen	Tag
		MH/AZ	9.7.19...

Betreff
Bestellung Nummer CDZ/3497

Sehr geehrte Herren,

vor einer Woche haben wir Ihrem Vertreter, Herrn Georg Waldemann, die folgende
Bestellung erteilt:

Kaffee-Service 'Brasilia' × 150

Tee-Service 'Balmoral' × 150

Kaffee-Service 'Tropicana' × 60

Wir schreiben jetzt, um die Bestellung zu bestätigen und auch darauf hinzuweisen, daß
sorgfältige Verpackung der Waren erforderlich ist. Letztes Jahr bestellten wir ähnliche
Waren von einem anderen englischen Hersteller, und die Verpackung entsprach nicht
unseren Anforderungen. Die Porzellanwaren wurden mit dem Schiff transportiert und
wurden unterwegs beschädigt. Wir müssen deshalb auf Verpackung der Waren in Holzkisten
bestehen, und sie sollten mit Wellpappe oder Holzwolle verpackt werden. Um Schwierigkeiten
mit der Zollbehörde in Dover zu vermeiden, muß das Bruttogewicht auf jeder Kiste angegeben
werden.

Wir nehmen an, daß die Waren per Bahn und Schiff transportiert werden, und daß der von
Ihrem Vertreter angegebene Preis die Frachtkosten einschließt. Bitte teilen Sie uns mit, ob
Sie die Bestellung bis Ende Juli versandbereit haben können.

Wir hoffen auf baldige Antwort und verbleiben

mit freundlichen Grüßen

M. Haller
Leiter

(Multilingual Business Handbook skeleton: D68, D70, D78, D80, D81, D116, D48, D50, D56)

Ternby Porcelain plc
55–61 Denby Road
Stoke on Trent
England

Tel: 0782 645398
Telex: TERPOR 873048

18.7.19...

Your Reference: MH/AZ
Our Reference: SW/DL

Herrn
M. Haller
Gebr. Haller GmbH
Sesamstraße 87
8400 Regensburg
West Germany

Dear Mr Haller

We thank you for your letter of 9 July. You need not be concerned about the packaging of the goods you ordered, as it is our custom to wrap porcelain items in packing paper and corrugated cardboard, and to pack them in wooden crates. We should however point out that the crates are not returnable.

We usually send our goods by road to the port, and then by rail within Germany: we have many German customers, and we have found this the most convenient method, as the transport costs are somewhat lower. Alternatively, we could ship the goods by rail in England to the port, but this would involve a 10% increase in delivery costs. The price quoted by our representative does include freight costs.

There have been problems recently in Dover because of strikes by port workers, but we hope these will be resolved shortly. If this is the case, we can deliver the 'Brasilia' and 'Balmoral' services immediately. The remaining set will be ready for despatch in a week's time.

Yours sincerely

S. Walker

Export Sales Department

(*Multilingual Business Handbook skeleton:* D79, D80, D92, D94, D51, D48, D55, D56)

Continue the exchange of correspondence by composing a third letter (in German) on the basis of the following notes.

From: S. Walker (Ternby Porcelain)

To: M. Haller (Gebr. Haller)

- Thanks for letter.

- O.K. to send goods by road as outlined in your letter.

- We have received enquiry from customer in Saudi Arabia.

- Could you let me have a.s.a.p. cost of supplying 60 'Balmoral' tea services — by air freight — to Saudi Arabia.

- Delivery required within two weeks.

- Tricky, but if you can meet this deadline, larger orders will probably follow.

- Please let us have another 20 or 30 copies of your catalogue, as we have various business contacts who are interested.

SECTION 4:   INVOICES, PAYMENTS, REMINDERS

This section is based on terms and expressions contained in Section E of the *MULTILINGUAL BUSINESS HANDBOOK*.

SCHÜLER UND LEHRER
Fasanenstraße 46   6680 Neunkirchen

Telefon: 06821 2 38 93
Telex: 8454376

Style Pens
48 Hinnington Avenue

Canterbury

England

Ihr Zeichen	Ihre Nachricht vom	Unser Zeichen	Tag
		AD/NB	4.8.19...

Betreff
Rechnung Nummer EB28/4296

Sehr geehrte Herren,

die Kugelschreiber, die wir im Juni von Ihnen bestellt haben, sind gestern bei uns
eingetroffen, und wir haben heute Ihre Rechnung erhalten. Wir glauben aber, daß Sie sich
verrechnet haben. Als Ihr Vertreter Willi Alexis uns am 5. Mai besuchte, teilte er uns mit,
daß Sie für Erstaufträge einen Rabatt von 4% auf Ihre Katalogpreise gewähren. Dieser Rabatt
ist aber nicht von der Endsumme abgezogen worden. Wir sind überzeugt, daß dies auf einen
Fehler in Ihrer Rechnungsabteilung zurückzuführen ist, und wir wären Ihnen dankbar,
wenn Sie die Rechnung entsprechend berichtigen könnten.

Wir sehen Ihrer baldigen Antwort gern entgegen.

Mit freundlichen Grüßen

A. Dünen
Leiter

(*Multilingual Business Handbook skeleton:* E2, E4, E5, B128, B80, E16, E27, E22)

S T Y L E PENS
48 Hinnington Avenue
Canterbury

Tel: 0227 81943
Telex: STY 847637

12.8.88

Your Reference: AD/NB
Our Reference: DH/AL

Schüler und Lehrer
Fasanenstraße 46
6680 Neunkirchen
West Germany

Dear Mr Dünen

Thank you for your letter of 4 August, in which you draw our attention to our invoice number EB28/4296. I have to inform you that we did not in fact make a mistake in our invoice. The price quoted to you by our representative was for pens model 42/A in our summer catalogue. Unfortunately our stock of these pens is now exhausted. Since you required delivery of the pens urgently, we have sent you 500 pens model 46/C, which are better quality than the ones you ordered. The price is a little higher, and therefore the sum of £250 quoted on our invoice is correct.

We should be grateful if you could instruct your bank to pay this amount to our account as soon as possible.

Yours sincerely

D. Holeman

Accounts Department

(*Multilingual Business Handbook skeleton:* A10, B27, B18, D6, E70)

Continue the exchange of correspondence by composing a third letter (in German) on the basis of the following notes.

From: A. Dünen (Schüler und Lehrer)

To: D. Holeman (Style Pens)

- Thanks for your letter.

- We did not order pens model 46/C, but 42/A.

- We are not prepared to pay the higher price quoted.

- We shall therefore pay the amount of £210 to your account.

- Alternatively, we can return the pens.

- Please advise.

ANTON KRUGER AG
Hannoverallee 57-61   4600 Dortmund

Telefon: 0231 94 32 46
Telex: 822549

Leatherite
Holborne Circus

Birmingham

England

Ihr Zeichen	Ihre Nachricht vom	Unser Zeichen	Tag
		ON/GL	6.2.19...

Betreff
Zahlungsverzögerung – Bestellung Nummer AJB/2365

Sehr geehrte Herren,

vor drei Monaten haben Sie uns die folgende Bestellung erteilt:

50 Aktentaschen (Leder – braun)

120 Aktentaschen (Leder – schwarz)

Diese Waren wurden vor 6 Wochen geliefert, und wir erwarten noch Ihre Zahlung. Es kann sein, daß unsere Rechnung vielleicht verlorengegangen ist, und wir legen eine Kopie bei. Wir lenken Ihre Aufmerksamkeit auf die Tatsache, daß wir noch nicht den Restbetrag unseres Septemberauszugs erhalten haben.

Da diese fälligen Beträge seit langer Zeit offenstehen, müssen wir darauf bestehen, daß Sie uns den Grund für die Zahlungsverzögerung mitteilen.

In der Zwischenzeit haben wir eine weitere Bestellung für 150 Aktentaschen erhalten. Sie werden sicher verstehen, daß wir keine weiteren Aufträge ausführen können, bis die Rechnungen beglichen werden.

Mit freundlichen Grüßen

O. Nädel
Verkaufsleiter

(*Multilingual Business Handbook skeleton:* C6, E95, E99, B27, E98, E101, E100)

Leatherite
Holborne Circus
Birmingham B23 6FG

Tel: 021 335847
Telex: LEBRUM 38576

23.2.19...

Your Reference: ON/GL
Our Reference: HC/SC

Anton Kruger AG
Hannoverallee 57-61
4600 Dortmund
West Germany

Dear Sirs

We acknowledge receipt of your letter of 6 February. We regret the delay in payment of the
invoices to which you refer, but we hope you will understand our position.

Since we placed our original order with you three months ago, we have had certain
problems. An important customer of ours is in financial difficulties and has had to cancel a
very large order. This in turn has obviously caused us some financial problems, and we are
at the moment doing our best to settle our outstanding invoices by the end of next month.

In the meantime we have transferred to your account the sum of DM4000 in part payment
of our December order.

We assure you that you will receive full payment shortly.

Yours faithfully

H. Carter

Accounts Manager

(*Multilingual Business Handbook skeleton*: E125, H87, C51, A96, E97, E80)

Continue the exchange of correspondence by composing a third letter (in German) on the basis of the following notes:

From: O. Nädel (Anton Kruger AG)

To: H. Carter (Leatherite)

- Thanks for your letter of 23 February

- You say you have transferred DM4000 to us

- Not received, according to our bank

- Cannot accept delay any longer

- We are granting further period of 9 days in which to pay

- If payment not made in that time, we shall take legal steps

SECTION 5:   COMPLAINTS

This section is based on terms and expressions contained in Section F of the *MULTILINGUAL BUSINESS HANDBOOK*.

CASA NUESTRA
Baumgartenallee 57   7000 Stuttgart

Telefon: 0711 62 61 43
Telex: 7213458

Clenton Fabrics
42-46 Hazel Road

Leeds LS2 9PG

England

Ihr Zeichen	Ihre Nachricht vom	Unser Zeichen	Tag
		FB/RB	21.7.19...

Betreff
Auftrag Nummer BZ4238

Sehr geehrte Herren,

wir möchten auf einen Fehler in der Sendung hinweisen, die wir gestern von Ihnen erhalten haben. Unter der obengenannten Auftragnummer hatten wir Ihnen die folgende Bestellung erteilt:

50 Badeteppiche 70×140 cm. (rosa)

60 Badeteppiche (rund) 120 cm. Durchmesser (blau)

40 Badeteppiche 100×60 cm. (grau)

Statt der 50 rosa Badeteppiche, die wir bestellt hatten, haben Sie uns 90 geschickt. In der Sendung fehlten die grauen Badeteppiche. Dieser Fehler ist uns besonders peinlich, weil wir Kunden haben, die schon 2 Wochen auf diese Artikel warten.

Da unser Lagerbestand zu Ende geht, sind wir bereit, die 90 rosa Badeteppiche zu behalten, wären Ihnen aber verbunden, wenn Sie uns sobald wie möglich die bestellten grauen Teppiche schicken könnten.

Wir hoffen auf baldige Antwort und verbleiben

mit freundlichen Grüßen

F. Berger
Leiter

(*Multilingual Business Handbook skeleton:* F3, F11, F14, B17)

Clenton Fabrics
42-46 Hazel Road
Leeds LS2 9PG

Tel: 0532 285746
Telex: CLENFAB 475867

30.7.19...

Your Reference: FB/RB
Our Reference: GC/FN

Casa Nuestra
Baumgartenallee 57
7000 Stuttgart
West Germany

Dear Mr Berger

Thank you for your letter of 21 July with reference to our recent delivery of bath mats. Please accept our sincere apologies for the error in the consignment. It seems that the error occurred in our packing department.

Unfortunately, we have in stock only 20 grey mats in the size you ordered. We are sending these to you today, and you should receive them by the end of the week. The remaining 20 will be sent to you within ten days.

We are sorry that our consignment was unsatisfactory, and we are prepared to offer you a discount of 6% on our catalogue prices for this order.

Yours sincerely

G. Clenton

Managing Director

(*Multilingual Business Handbook skeleton:* A10, F67, B20, F71, F72, B80)

Continue the exchange of correspondence by composing a third letter (in German) on the basis of the following notes.

From: F. Berger (Casa Nuestra)

To: G. Clenton (Clenton Fabrics)

- Thanks for letter.

- The consignment of 20 grey mats now arrived.

- Because of demand, we need further supply of 150 grey mats.

- In view of size of order, possible to grant discount?

- Please send autumn/winter catalogue as soon as it is ready.

Haus und Garten
Adenauerallee 36   4290 Bocholt

Telefon: 02871 423693
Telex: 493 2148

G. Delaney and Son

Unit 53

Barrymore Industrial Estate

Dover

England

Ihr Zeichen	Ihre Nachricht vom	Unser Zeichen	Tag
		OT/GL	14.8.19...

Betreff

Fehlerhafte Rasenmäher – Bestellung Nummer BDS/3857

Sehr geehrte Herren,

im Mai haben wir von Ihnen die folgenden Artikel bestellt:

30 Elektrorasenmäher 'Garden Star' (mit Stahlblechgehäuse)

25 Benzin-Rasenmäher 'Premier' mit Selbstantrieb.

Obwohl wir auf Lieferung binnen 3 Wochen bestanden hatten, haben wir erst gestern die Mäher erhalten, und wir bedauern, uns über die Sendung beschweren zu müssen. Bei 10 Benzinmähern fehlten die Zündkerzen, und bei 7 Elektromähern war die Fangbox beschädigt. Wir glauben, daß die Waren durch unsachgemäße Behandlung beschädigt wurden. Bei weiteren 8 Mähern war das Gehäuse verkratzt. Fünf Elektromäher weisen schon Rost auf, obwohl alle Mäher eine 10 Jahre Garantie auf Durchrostung haben.

Wir müssen darauf bestehen, daß Sie alle fehlerhaften Maschinen ersetzen oder uns den Wert der beschädigten Waren gutschreiben. Diese Angelegenheit hat uns erhebliche Schwierigkeiten bereitet, da wir die Waren dringend brauchen. Ausnahmsweise könnten wir die Maschinen mit beschädigter Fangbox behalten, aber wir könnten sie natürlich nur zu einem erheblich reduzierten Preis verkaufen. Wir müßten in diesem Fall auf einem Rabatt von 50% auf den Katalogpreis bestehen.

Wir sehen Ihrer Stellungnahme gern entgegen.

Mit freundlichen Grüßen

O. Thesaurus
Verkaufsleiter

(Multilingual Business Handbook skeleton: F2, F19, F32, F47, F57, F36, F46)

G. Delaney and Son

Garden Machines and Tools
Unit 53
Barrymore Industrial Estate
Dover
Kent

Tel: 0304 423693
Telex: DELSON 38574

23.8.19...

Your Reference: OT/GL
Our Reference: GD/AB

Herrn
O. Thesaurus
Haus und Garten
Adenauerallee 36
4290 Bocholt
West Germany

Dear Mr Thesaurus

Thank you for your letter of 14 August. We are sorry to hear that the consignment of mowers we sent to you was unsatisfactory, but we cannot understand why this should be the case. We check all our machines very carefully before despatch, and the items sent to you were in good condition when despatched. We can only assume that they must have been damaged in transit, and we therefore suggest that you take up the matter with the haulage company in question. We cannot accept responsibility for damage of this kind.

You mention that several of the mowers had no spark plugs, and we are sending these to you under separate cover. We apologise for this oversight. We shall of course replace at our cost the mowers which show signs of rust, since this is, as you point out, covered by our guarantee. We should be grateful if you could return these particular mowers to us as soon as possible so that we may inspect them ourselves.

When you have contacted the haulage company, perhaps you could let us have a report from them detailing the damage? This is the first time we have used this company, and we would obviously wish to avoid similar problems in the future. We hope we have been of assistance to you in this matter, and apologise for any inconvenience caused.

Yours sincerely

George Delaney (Managing Director)

(Multilingual Business Handbook skeleton: F71, F74, E3, F27, F61, F76, F70, F64, F82, F62)

Continue the exchange of correspondence by composing a third letter (in German) on the basis of the following notes.

From: O. Thesaurus (Haus und Garten)

To: G. Delaney and Son

- Cannot accept that you are not responsible for damage caused in transit.

- Your responsibility to ensure goods arrive in good condition.

- You should make further enquiries with haulier.

- We shall retain goods in the meantime.

- Shall also withhold full payment until matter settled.

- You will shortly receive payment for the machines which arrived in good condition.

SECTION 6:   AGENCIES/REPS

This section is based on terms and expressions contained in Section G of the *MULTILINGUAL BUSINESS HANDBOOK*.

MÖBEL GRUEN GmbH
Deteringstraße 45 4400 Münster

Stilson Marketing
43 White Mews

Reading

England

Telefon: 0251 8 03 28
Telex: 251349

Ihr Zeichen	Ihre Nachricht vom	Unser Zeichen	Tag
		OR/DT	14.6.19...

Betreff
Vertretung – GB

Sehr geehrte Herren,

wir sind eine mittelgroße Firma, und wir sind auf die Herstellung von Büromöbel spezialisiert, insbesondere die Herstellung von Schreibtischen und Computertischen. Ihr Name wurde uns von Geschäftsfreunden gegeben, da wir einen Vertreter in Großbritannien für unser neues Sortiment suchen. Wir glauben, daß Sie beträchtliche Erfahrung in dem Verkauf von Artikeln dieser Art besitzen, und daß Sie schon mehrere französische und belgische Firmen vertreten.

Wir haben schon Kunden in England, die seit Jahren Möbel von uns beziehen, aber Ihre Aufgabe würde darin bestehen, den Markt für uns auszuweiten. Wir glauben, daß unsere Waren einen guten Absatz in Schottland finden würden, wenn wir den dortigen Markt intensiv bearbeiten könnten.

Wir würden Ihnen selbstverständlich unser deutsches Werbematerial zur Verfügung stellen, aber dieses Material müßte ins Englische übersetzt werden. Wenn Sie es vorziehen, könnten wir selbst die Übersetzung veranlassen.

Wir hoffen, daß Sie Interesse an dieser Vertretung haben und sehen Ihrer Antwort gern entgegen.

Mit freundlichen Grüßen

O. Raidt
Leiter

(*Multilingual Business Handbook skeleton:* B2, A15, G14, ,G19, G44, G66, G65)

Stilson Marketing
43 White Mews
Reading

Tel: 0743 462839
Telex: STIL 349246

25.6.19...

Your Reference: OT/DT
Our Reference: MS/NA

Herrn
O. Raidt
Möbel Grün GmbH
Deteringstraße 45
4400 Münster
West Germany

Dear Mr Raidt

Thank you very much for your letter of 14 June. As you are already aware, we are very experienced in this type of work, and we successfully represent many similar firms. You say that you are interested in developing the market for your goods in Scotland. I am pleased to inform you that we have good connections with various large stores in Glasgow, Edinburgh and Aberdeen, so we do not anticipate any problems in this respect.

We too are sure that your goods will find a ready market in this country, and we should be pleased to take on the agency for your products. We should like to clarify a couple of points first of all, however:

We assume that as far as Great Britain is concerned, we shall be the sole agents for your goods. With regard to the advertising material: we can arrange translation of this, but it would of course have to be at your expense.

Could you also let us know what commission will be payable, and whether this would be payable on all orders from this area?

We look forward to hearing from you again.

Yours sincerely

Martin Stilson
Senior Partner

(*Multilingual Business Handbook skeleton*: G40, G42, G43, G38, G23, G65, G67, G91)

Continue the exchange of correspondence by composing a third letter (in German) on the basis of the following notes.

From: O. Raidt (Möbel Grün)

To: M. Stilson (Stilson Marketing)

- Thanks for expression of interest in agency.

- We are in agreement with your arranging of translation material at our expense.

- We enclose a sample German catalogue — please inform us of approximate cost of translation into English.

- Our proposed rate of commission is 5%.

- This would be payable on all orders from your area — payable quarterly.

- You would be sole agents for GB.

- Please inform us by end of month of these terms are acceptable.

AGENTUR FLINK
Untere Bergstraße 46 6600 Saarbrücken

Telefon: 0681 48 32 63
Telex: 4423596

Holgreave Domestic Appliances
36-40 Belgrade Avenue

Harrogate

England

Ihr Zeichen	Ihre Nachricht vom	Unser Zeichen	Tag
		GF/DL	6.3.19...

Betreff
Bewerbung um Vertretung

Sehr geehrte Herren,

von Geschäftsfreunden haben wir erfahren, daß Sie Hersteller von Waschautomaten und Spülmaschinen sind, und daß Sie einen Vertreter für Deutschland suchen. Wir möchten uns um die Vertretung Ihrer Produkte bewerben. Unsere Agentur wurde vor 20 Jahren gegründet, und wir spezialisieren uns auf den Absatz von Elektro-Haushaltgeräten. Wir haben Ausstellungsräume in Saarbrücken und in Metz — wir wären deshalb auch in der Lage, den französischen Markt für Sie zu bearbeiten, da wir ein weites Netz von Geschäftsbeziehungen in Frankreich haben. Zur Zeit sind wir keinem anderen britischen Hersteller verpflichtet.

Für den Verkauf von Elektrogeräten sind Fachkenntnisse erforderlich, und wir haben fünf Fachvertreter hier in Saarbrücken und drei in Metz — wir haben keine nebenberuflichen Vertreter. Alle Vertreter, die für uns arbeiten, bilden wir selbst aus. Wir wären auch in der Lage, den Kundendienst in Deutschland und Frankreich für Sie zu übernehmen.

Unsere gewöhnliche Provisionsrate beträgt 12%, und diese Provision wird auf alle Aufträge aus unserem Gebiet erteilt. Wir sind überzeugt, daß Ihre Waren einen guten Absatz in Deutschland finden werden, und wir hoffen, daß Sie daran interessiert sind, uns die Vertretung Ihrer Erzeugnisse für Deutschland und Frankreich zu übertragen.

Wir sehen Ihrer Antwort gern entgegen und verbleiben

mit freundlichen Grüßen

G. Flink
Leiter

(*Multilingual Business Handbook skeleton:* G39, G41, G44, G49, G46, G8, G30, G45, G79, G38)

HOLGREAVE DOMESTIC APPLIANCES
Belgrade Avenue Harrogate

Tel: 0423 389245
FAX: 0423 44 88 99

Your Reference:	GF/DL	15.3.19...
Our Reference:	DT/LN	

Agentur Flink
Untere Bergstraße 46
6600 Saarbrücken
West Germany

Dear Sirs

We thank you for your letter of 6 March, in which you ask about the possibility of taking on the agency for our products in Germany and France. As far as the French market is concerned, we have already concluded an agency agreement with another company, but we might well be interested in granting you the German agency.

I should point out that we find your commission rate rather high. To our French agents we pay a commission of 8%, and this is payable on all orders placed through them or their intermediaries. Since the commission rate you quote is considerably higher than this, I assume that publicity material is provided by yourselves at your expense. If this is the case, then I am sure that we can come to some sort of compromise regarding the commission rate. I shall be coming to Germany myself in about three weeks' time, and I can discuss the matter with you then.

If we do grant you the agency, it will of course be on a trial basis for the first year, and thereafter we should be in a position to grant you the sole selling rights for Germany. I should be interested to hear if you would be in a position to take on an agency for the GDR for us, as we are thinking of expanding our market to include Eastern Europe.

I hope to be in Saarbrücken on or about the 10 April, and should be grateful if you would let me know if you are available then. When we meet we can perhaps clarify some of the points I raise in this letter.

I look forward to hearing from you.

Yours sincerely

David Tonks (Sales Manager)

(Multilingual Business Handbook skeleton: G60, G61, G80, G66, G67, G56, G57)

Continue the exchange of correspondence by composing a third letter (in German) on the basis of the following notes.

From: G. Flink (Agentur Flink)

To: D. Tonks (Holgreave Domestic Appliances)

- I shall be available on morning of 10 April.

- Ring when you arrive at station — we'll pick you up.

- We have a linked agency in Leipzig, so could help with the GDR market — further details when we meet.

- We do provide publicity material at our expense, hence the higher commission rate.

- Not too happy with the idea of a one-year trial period — reduce this to 6 months?

- How long is contract with French agency valid? We should be interested in taking it over after expiry.

- Look forward to seeing you in April.

SECTION 7:   REFERENCES

This section is based on terms and expressions contained in Section G of the *MULTILINGUAL BUSINESS HANDBOOK*.

DEMA Versicherung
Lübkestraße 42 6900 Heidelberg

Telefon: 06221 2 36 45
Telex: 461643

Herrn
R. Hart
Staveley Engineering
Unit 46
Beldroy Industrial Estate

Leeds

England

Ihr Zeichen	Ihre Nachricht vom	Unser Zeichen	Tag
		DM/LD	4.5.19...

Betreff
Referenz

Sehr geehrter Herr Hart,

Fräulein Lisa James hat sich um die Stelle als Fremdsprachenkorrespondentin bei unserer Versicherungsgesellschaft beworben und hat Sie als Referenz angegeben. Ich wäre Ihnen dankbar, wenn Sie mir Auskünfte über ihren Charakter und ihre Fähigkeiten geben könnten.

Ich möchte darauf hinweisen, das diese Position hohe Anforderungen stellt, und daß wir eine Mitarbeiterin suchen, die besonders anpassungsfähig ist, da sie in verschiedenen Abteilungen arbeiten muß.

Ihre Auskunft werden wir selbstverständlich mit größter Verschwiegenheit behandeln. Die Vorstellungsgespräche für diese Stelle finden am 15. Juni statt. Ich sehe Ihrer baldigen Antwort gern entgegen und verbleibe

mit freundlichen Grüßen

Doris Mühlbach
Personalleiterin

(*Multilingual Business Handbook skeleton:* H1, H2, H3, H4, H8, H10)

Staveley Engineering
Unit 46
Beldroy Industrial Estate
Leeds

Tel: 0532 235648
Telex: STAV 847564

14.5.19...

Your Reference: DM/LD
Our Reference:RH/AN

Frau
Doris Mühlbach
Dema Versicherung
Lübkestraße 42
6900 Heidelberg
West Germany

Dear Ms Mühlbach

Thank you for your letter of 4 May requesting information on Miss Lisa James.

As you will already know from her application, Miss James is a graduate of Newcastle University, and she subsequently completed a course for bilingual secretaries at St Lucia College, Basildon. She has worked for us since completing her course there. She has been employed in our sales and marketing department, and has been responsible for all our correspondence with our French and German suppliers and customers.

She is an efficient worker and is totally reliable. Her work is always of the highest quality. At present the promotion possibilities in our company are for several reasons limited, and it is probably for this reason that Miss James has applied for the post with you. I know that she also wishes to work abroad to make better use of her knowledge of foreign languages. Should she be successful in obtaining the post with you we should be sorry to lose her, and I have no hesitation in recommending her to you.

Yours sincerely

R. Hart

Accounts Manager

(Multilingual Business Handbook skeleton: H13, H20, H21, H45, H28, H27, H47)

Continue the exchange of correspondence by composing a third letter (in German) on the basis of the following notes.

From: D. Mühlbach (Dema Versicherung)

To: R. Hart (Staveley Engineering)

- Thanks for providing reference.

- Miss Jones appears to be one of best candidates for post — will probably offer her the job.

- But – 3 quick queries:

- What is her current salary?

- She indicates on her application form some health problems recently — have these affected her work?

- Does your company have its own pension scheme? If so, please send details — they are needed for our personnel department if she gets the post.

MASCHINENBAU REINHARDT
Augustenstraße 43 5400 Koblenz

Telefon: 0261 3 42 63
Telex: 862434

G. & L. Jeffreys
36-40 Windon Rise

Bristol

England

Ihr Zeichen	Ihre Nachricht vom	Unser Zeichen	Tag
		DB/NW	2.2.19...

Betreff
Referenz

Sehr geehrte Herren,

wir sind Hersteller von Kurbel- und Nockenwellen für die Autoindustrie, und die Firma Dayton Automotive Engineering in Bristol hat uns gerade einen großen Auftrag im Wert von DM45 000 erteilt. Die Firma hat uns gebeten, ihr einen Kredit einzuräumen und hat Ihren Namen als Referenz angegeben.

Da wir zum ersten Mal mit dieser Firma handeln, wären wir für Auskünfte über ihre finanzielle Lage dankbar. Könnten wir, nach Ihrer Meinung, ihr einen Kredit in Höhe von DM30 000 einräumen? Für Auskunft über ihre Zuverläßigkeit und Konkurrenzfähigkeit wären wir auch besonders dankbar.

Selbstverständlich werden wir Ihre Auskunft streng vertraulich behandeln. Wir sehen Ihrer baldigen Antwort gern entgegen und verbleiben

mit freundlichen Grüßen

D. Behmer
Finanzleiter

(*Multilingual Business Handbook skeleton:* H55, H57, H59, H69, H66, H63, H72)

G. & L. Jeffreys
36–40 Windon Rise
Bristol

Tel: 0272 43 98 66
Telex: BRISJEF 846374

12.2.19...

Your Reference: DB/NW
Our Reference: MC/LS

Herrn
D. Behmer
Maschinenbau Reinhardt
Augustenstraße 43
5400 Koblenz
West Germany

Dear Mr Behmer

We thank you for your letter of 2 February in which you ask for information on Dayton Automotive Engineering. The situation with regard to this company is a rather difficult and complex one. The company was founded at least 40 years ago, and is a well-established firm in this area. We ourselves have done business with them for about twelve years, and until last year we found them to be completely reliable in fulfilling their financial obligations.

Last year we had to send several reminders to the company, and although our invoices have now been settled, we believe that they may be in a difficult financial position. As we have not traded with them since November of last year, we feel that we are in the circumstances not able to advise you further. We suggest you contact G. Huyton and Son, Langtree Road, Exeter, who have done a lot of business with Dayton in the last two years. If their impressions of the company concur with ours, we would advise you to be cautious in granting credit.

Yours sincerely

Miles Cooke

Finance/Accounts Department

(*Multilingual Business Handbook skeleton:* I1, H75, H81, H82, H84, H86, H87, H95, H90)

Continue the exchange of correspondence by composing a third letter (in German) on the basis of the following notes.

From: D. Behmer (Maschinenbau Reinhardt)

To: G. Huyton and Son

- We have been referred to you by Jeffreys.

- We need information on trading/financial position of Dayton.

- Information from Jeffreys not clear.

- Appears that recently, Dayton have had financial problems.

- What is your recent experience with the company?

- Would you risk credit?

- Please give early reply — we have to make decision urgently.

SECTION 8: JOB APPLICATIONS AND ADVERTISEMENTS

This section is based on terms and expressions contained in Section I of the *MULTILINGUAL BUSINESS HANDBOOK*.

Wir suchen zum nächstmöglichen Termin eine englische oder deutsche Mitarbeiterin als **zweisprachige Fremdsprachenkorrespondentin** für unsere Exportabteilung.

Wir brauchen für diese verantwortungsvolle Position eine gewandte und kontaktfähige Mitarbeiterin, die in der Lage ist, alle Sekretariatsarbeiten selbständig zu erledigen. Für diese Stelle sind hervorragende Englisch- und Deutschkenntnisse erforderlich. Weitere Fremdsprachenkenntnisse (z.B. Französisch oder Spanisch) wären von Vorteil.

Wir bieten Ihnen angenehme Arbeitsbedingungen, ein gutes Gehalt und alle sozialen Leistungen. Wenn Sie an dieser Stelle Interesse haben, setzen Sie sich bitte in Verbindung mit unserem Personalleiter, Herrn Wolfgang Linz, Hamann und Dietze AG, Lindenbergstraße 36, 6900 Heidelberg.

45 Winchester Avenue
Manchester M43 9TF
England

5.4.19...

Herrn W. Linz
Hamann und Dietze AG
Lindenbergstraße 36
6900 Heidelberg
West Germany

Dear Mr Linz

I see from your advertisement in the English and German press that you are looking for a bilingual secretary for your export department, and I wish to apply for this post.

I am currently working for an export firm in Manchester, but both for personal reasons and also to improve my career prospects, I wish to change my position.

I went to University in Leeds, where I studied German as my main subject and Spanish as subsidiary. I have used both languages in my present post, and I have considerable experience of working with microcomputers and word-processors.

I should be grateful if you could send me further details of the post together with an application form.

Yours sincerely

Catherine Wilkes

(*Multilingual Business Handbook skeleton:* I42, I45, I52, I58, I61, I54, I78, I79, I71, I72, I46, I47)

Continue the exchange of correspondence by composing a third letter (in German) on the basis of the following notes.

From: W. Linz (Hamann und Dietze)

To: C. Wilkes

- We do not have application forms as such.

- Please send detailed letter of application — three copies.

- Send curriculum vitae in German.

- Quote two referees.

- Interviews for the post will take place at beginning of May.

Wir sind ein bedeutendes Unternehmen für Elektrogeräte und suchen einen erfahrenen Verkaufsingenieur für unsere neue Niederlassung in Marburg. Für diese bedeutende Position brauchen wir einen Mitarbeiter/eine Mitarbeiterin zwischen 25 und 35, mit mindestens 5 Jahren Berufserfahrung auf diesem Gebiet. Deutsch- und Englischkenntnisse sind für diese Stelle erforderlich.

Das Gehalt erfolgt nach Alter und Berufserfahrung, beträgt aber nicht weniger als DM6000 monatlich.

Sollten Sie an dieser Stelle Interesse haben, richten Sie Ihre Bewerbung (in englischer oder deutscher Sprache) mit den üblichen Unterlagen an unseren Personalleiter, Anton Frank, Elektro Herder GmbH, Oppenheimer Straße 27, 7500 Karlsruhe.

42 The Croft
Lichfield
England

3.7.19...

Herrn
Anton Frank
Elektro Herder GmbH
Oppenheimer Straße 27
7500 Karlsruhe
West Germany

Dear Sir

I see from your recent advertisement in the trade press that you are looking for a sales engineer for your Marburg branch, and I am interested in applying for this post.

As you will see from the enclosed curriculum vitae I am a graduate of the University of London, where I read Engineering with German as an optional subsidiary subject. I spent six months of my course with an engineering company in Germany. You will also see that after graduating I worked for four years in Germany, and I speak and write the language fluently.

I have worked for my present company, Keyway Electrical plc, for several years, and I am currently in charge of their sales department, specialising in the sale of electrical equipment to industry. Although I find my present work interesting, I very much enjoyed my period of work in Germany, and I now wish to find a permanent post there with a large organisation such as yours.

The following have agreed to act as referees on my behalf:

1) Dr Edith Kosloska, Dürer und Albrecht AG, Meersburger Straße 43, 8070 Ingolstadt.

2) Dr Dieter Frank, Christofstraße 22, 3540 Korbach.

I should be pleased to provide you with any further information you may require, but should be grateful if you would not approach my current employers at the present time. I should point out at this stage that, should you wish to invite me for interview, I shall be in the United States from 29 July to 15 August inclusive.

Yours faithfully

Lionel Hurst
Enc.

(Multilingual Business Handbook skeleton: I142, I145, I148, I177, I180, I178, I164, I155, I1107, I1102, I191)

CURRICULUM VITAE

NAME	Lionel Geoffrey HURST
ADDRESS	42 The Croft Lichfield Staffordshire England
DATE OF BIRTH	4.5.58
PLACE OF BIRTH	Winchester
SCHOOL EDUCATION	1962-68 Primary School in Winchester 1968-76 Secondary School in Bath Ordinary Level subjects passed: French, German, Physics, Maths, Chemistry, Biology, English Language. Advanced Level subjects passed: Physics, Maths, Chemistry.
UNIVERSITY EDUCATION	1976-80 University of London Subjects studied: Main: Engineering (electrical) Subsidiary: German, Maths. Sept. '78 – Feb. '79 Work experience with Dürer & Albrecht AG, Ingolstadt, as integral part of undergraduate course. Degree obtained: BSc. (Hons), 2(i).
PROFESSIONAL EXPERIENCE	1980 – 1984 Engineer with Dürer & Albrecht AG, Ingolstadt (in quality control department) 1984 – present: Sales Engineer with Keyway Electrical, Walsall.
KNOWLEDGE OF FOREIGN LANGUAGES	Fluent German, basic French.
INTERESTS	Photography, Cycling, Squash, Travel.

Continue the exchange of correspondence by composing a third letter (in German) on the basis of the following notes.

From: Anton Frank (Personnel Manager, Elektro Herder)

To: Lionel Hurst

- Thank you for your application for the post.

- We have written to your referees already.

- Won't contact your employers yet.

- Please send us more information on type of work done at Keyway, as we can't get this information from references.

- Interviews to be held in August, so can you revise your travel plans?

- Inform a.s.a.p.

SECTION 9: CHANGE OF ADDRESS etc.

This section is based on terms and expressions contained in Section J of the *MULTILINGUAL BUSINESS HANDBOOK*.

Leder-Shop
Balzer Straße 36   4000 Düsseldorf

Telefon: 0211 35 48 69
Telex: 8586391

Spears Leather Goods
24 Hill Tree Avenue

Newcastle-upon-Tyne

England

Ihr Zeichen	Ihre Nachricht vom	Unser Zeichen WK/NL	Tag 4.2.19...

Betreff
Bestellung auf Ledertaschen

Sehr geehrte Herren,

vor einem Jahr belieferten Sie uns mit 200 Ledertaschen (Modell 'Verona') für unser Geschäft hier in Düsseldorf. Wegen großer Nachfrage von unseren Kunden während der Weihnachtszeit haben wir nur noch 15 solche Taschen auf Lager. Wir möchten Ihnen deshalb die folgende Bestellung erteilen:

250 Ledertaschen (Modell 'Verona') Bestell-Nummer LB4328

150 Ledertaschen – weiß (Model 'Primavera') Bestell-Nummer LB6293.

Die Bestellung basiert auf Ihren Katalogpreisen, d.h. £9 pro Tasche für Artikel Nr LB4328 und £11 pro Tasche für Artikel Nr LB6293. Wir benötigen die Waren binnen 3 Wochen.

Ich wäre Ihnen verbunden, wenn Sie diese Bestellung und die oben angegebenen Preise sobald wie möglich bestätigen würden.

Mit freundlichen Grüßen

Wilfried Karmann
Leiter

(Multilingual Business Handbook skeleton: B56, B20, C6, C63)

Spears Leather Goods
24 Hill Tree Avenue
Newcastle-upon-Tyne
England

Tel: 0632 432962
Telex: SPEA 43249

16.3.19...

Your Reference: WK/NL
Our Reference: MT/OL

Herrn
W. Karmann
Leder-Shop
Balzer Straße 36
4000 Düsseldorf
West Germany

Dear Mr Karmann

Thank you for your letter of 2 February. Please excuse the delay in replying to your letter, which only reached me two days ago. I have to write to inform you that because of the growth in our business we have now opened a new factory in Sunderland, which has taken over the manufacture of the goods which you wish to order. The address of the new factory is: 36 Boston Hall Road, Sunderland, tel: 0783 754639 (contact Mr James Walker).

You should in future forward any correspondence relating to handbag orders to this address, and inform your purchase department accordingly.

The factory in Newcastle now specialises only in the manufacture of jackets and coats. I apologise for any inconvenience this change of address has caused, but can assure you that we shall now be able to give better service to all our customers. I have passed your order on to our new factory, and you should receive the goods you ordered within two weeks.

Yours sincerely

Martin Tyler

Sales/Despatch Department

(*Multilingual Business Handbook skeleton:* J4, J3, J10, J11, J21, J6)

Continue the exchange of correspondence by composing a third letter (in German) on the basis of the following notes.

From: Wilfried Karmann (Leder-Shop)

To: James Walker (Spears Leather Goods — Sunderland branch)

- We have received letter from Martin Tyler indicating change of address.

- Have in meantime received the goods we ordered.

- The prices on the invoice were about 6% higher than anticipated, but no indication why.

- Please confirm correct price, and send new catalogue with up-to-date prices.

- Do you have separate catalogues for clothing and bags? If so, please send both.

Ketterer AG

Tannenstraße 45   7530 Pforzheim

Telefon: 07231 2 60 36
Telex: 3645867

Dyson Automart
Unit 54
Lonsdale Trading Park

Luton

England

Ihr Zeichen	Ihre Nachricht vom	Unser Zeichen	Tag
		AK/DL	14.7.19...

Betreff
Ihre Bestellung Nummer NL4238

Sehr geehrte Herren,

wir danken Ihnen für Ihre Bestellung vom 10. Juni auf

120 Stahlgürtelreifen – Größe 175HR14

140 Stahlgürtelreifen – Größe 195/70HR14.

Wir bedauern, Ihnen mitzuteilen, daß wir diese Reifen nicht mehr herstellen. Wir sind von der Firma Dollinger und Flederer übernommen worden, die ihren Hauptsitz in München hat, und unsere Fabrik hier in Pforzheim wird im September stillgelegt.

Wir schlagen vor, daß Sie sich mit dieser Firma bezüglich künftiger Bestellungen in Verbindung setzen. Die Adresse ist: Antoniusstraße 48, 8000 München 1, Telefonnummer 089 55 79 15. Der Verkaufsleiter heißt Wolfgang Kempinski.

Wir hoffen, Ihnen mit dieser Information gedient zu haben und verbleiben

mit freundlichen Grüßen

Anton Ketterer
Inhaber

(*Multilingual Business Handbook skeleton:* A31, J19, J29, J23, J25, J27, A126)

Dyson Automart
Unit 54
Lonsdale Trading Estate
Luton
England

Tel: 0582 856453
Telex: DYS 362491

28.7.19...

Your Reference: AK/DL
Our Reference: JT/LL

Herrn
Wolfgang Kempinski
Dollinger und Flederer
Antoniusstraße 48
8000 München 1

Dear Mr Kempinski

We recently wrote to the tyre manufacturers Reifen Ketterer to order a number of radial tyres for our unit here in Luton. We have placed regular orders with this firm for several years now, and I was surprised to learn from them that they are ceasing production at their Pforzheim plant. We were referred to you by Herr Ketterer, as you are the company which has taken them over. We wish to order the following:

120 Steel radial tyres (size 175HR14)

140 Steel radial tyres (size 195/70 HR14)

The price indicated in the Ketterer catalogue is DM65 for the smaller size, and DM88 for the larger. As there has already been a delay, we now require the goods within twelve days. Please let us know if you cannot deliver within this period.

We also had, in a consignment received from Ketterer recently, a number of faulty tyres — twenty in all. Since you have now taken over their production, we shall be returning these to you in the next week, and ask you to credit us with the value of the faulty items.

Yours sincerely

John Taylor (Manager)

(Multilingual Business Handbook skeleton: B30, J20, C6, C14, C15, F10, F57)

Continue the exchange of correspondence by composing a third letter (in German) on the basis of the following notes.

From: Wolfgang Kempinski (Dollinger und Flederer)

To: J. Taylor (Dyson Automart)

- We can deliver the tyres you ordered within the specified time.

- Prices have now changed — DM72 for 175 size, DM93 for 195 size.

- Please confirm by 'phone if acceptable.

- In actual fact Ketterer are responsible for faulty tyres — they will still be trading in Stuttgart, producing other goods.

- Have passed letter on to them for reimbursement re faulty tyres.

- You should be hearing from them shortly.

SECTION 10:   TRAVEL AND HOTEL RESERVATIONS

This section is based on terms and expressions contained in Section K of the *MULTILINGUAL BUSINESS HANDBOOK*.

HELLER AG

Neuwiedstraße 45   8730 Bad Kissingen

Telefon: 0971 12 66
Telex: 672943

Drayton Hotel
43 Lichfield Road

Birmingham B22 9GH

England

Ihr Zeichen	Ihre Nachricht vom	Unser Zeichen AB/DK	Tag 4.3.19...

Betreff
Zimmerreservierung

Sehr geehrte Herren,

mit zwei Kollegen fahre ich im April zu einer Messe in Birmingham, und ich wäre Ihnen dankbar, wenn Sie mir mitteilen könnten, ob Sie vom 14. bis zum 18. April drei Einzelzimmer (mit Bad) frei haben.

Bitte teilen Sie mir den Preis eines Einzelzimmers für drei Übernachtungen (mit Frühstück) mit. Da wir ein großes Unternehmen mit vielen Arbeitnehmern und Agenturen sind, haben wir vor, im Herbst eine Konferenz für unsere Vertreter und Verkaufsingenieure in England zu veranstalten. Ihr Hotel wurde uns von Kollegen in der Branche als geeigneter Tagungsort vorgeschlagen. Ich wäre Ihnen verbunden, wenn Sie mir weitere Informationen über die Konferenzeinrichtungen in Ihrem Hotel würden zukommen lassen. Ich vermute, daß etwa 70 Personen an einer solchen Konferenz teilnehmen würden.

Mit freundlichen Grüßen

Anton Biederstein
Exportleiter

(*Multilingual Business Handbook skeleton:* K61, K66, K78)

Drayton Hotel
43 Lichfield Road
Birmingham B22 9GH

Tel: 021 438 2464

Your Reference: AB/DK
Our Reference: MB/DN

11.3.19...

Herrn
Anton Biederstein
Heller AG
Neuwiedstraße 45
8730 Bad Kissingen
West Germany

Dear Mr Biederstein

Thank you for your letter of 4 March. I am pleased to inform you that we do have three single rooms available for the period you require (14-18 April). We have two rooms with bath and toilet, and one room with shower and toilet. All of our rooms have colour TV, telephone and minibar. The inclusive price for four nights with breakfast is as follows:

room with bath/toilet £245

room with shower/toilet £220.

I should be grateful if you could let me know within 8 days if you wish to make the reservation.

You ask about conference facilities at our hotel. Our new brochure is being printed, and I shall send you a copy as soon as it is ready. Our hotel has two conference rooms, one for 60 people, and one for 120. The cost of the smaller room is £120 per day, the cost of the larger one is £165. If you require further information before you receive the brochure, please contact me again.

Yours sincerely

Michael Beardesley

Reservations Manager

(*Multilingual Business Handbook skeleton:* A32, K65, K83)

Continue the exchange of correspondence by composing a third letter (in German) on the basis of the following notes.

From: Anton Biederstein (Heller AG)

To: Michael Beardesley (Drayton Hotel)

- Thanks for your letter of 11 March.

- We wish to reserve the rooms.

- We must, however, change our departure date.

- Will now arrive on 15, leave on 19 April.

- Same price applies?

- Confirm if O.K.

- Please give details of travel from airport to hotel.

- Will await arrival of brochure before making further conference arrangements.

DÜRER-GYMNASIUM
Rosenheimer Landstraße 42   3510 Münden

Telefon: 05541 44 82

F.J. Riley
School Tours Specialists
44 Avon Avenue

Stratford

England

Ihr Zeichen	Ihre Nachricht vom	Unser Zeichen	Tag
		DH/MM	4.5.19...

Betreff
Reiseprogramm – Sommer 19..

Sehr geehrte Herren,

von Kollegen an einer anderen Schule habe ich erfahren, daß Sie Gruppenreisen in Mittelengland für ausländische Schüler organisieren. Wir haben es vor, mit einer Gruppe von etwa 30 Abiturienten nach England zu fahren, um Stratford und Evesham zu besuchen, mit einem 2- oder 3tägigen Ausflug nach London.

Aus Ihrem Sommerkatalog für letztes Jahr ersehe ich, daß Sie individuelle Reiseprogramme zusammenstellen können. Wir könnten Ende Juli nach England fahren, und wir würden wahrscheinlich 2 Wochen bleiben. Damit die Gesamtkosten nicht zu hoch sind, schlage ich vor, daß wir entweder mit dem Bus oder mit dem Zug fahren.

Für Ihre Vorschläge wäre ich Ihnen dankbar. Ich sehe Ihrer Antwort gern entgegen und verbleibe

mit freundlichen Grüßen

D. Hoeneß
Oberstudienrat

(Multilingual Business Handbook skeleton: A77)

F.J. Riley
Specialists in School Tours
44 Avon Avenue
Stratford
England

Tel: 0789 342643
Telex: STRIL 434296

Your Reference: DH/MM
Our Reference: FR/ML

12.5.19...

Herrn
D. Hoeneß
Dürer-Gymnasium
Rosenheimer Landstraße 42
3510 Münden
West Germany

Dear Mr Hoeneß

Thank you very much for your enquiry of 4 May regarding the possibility of a school trip for your pupils. In fact we organised a very similar holiday for a school party from Hannover last year, which proved most successful, and we feel that you may be interested in a comparable programme.

You and your pupils would travel to Ostend by train (we could book the whole journey for you) and then take to ferry to Dover. In Dover our coach would pick you up at the port and drive you to Stratford, where you would spend a week in twin-bedded rooms in a hotel in the mid price range. At the end of the first week you would transfer to Evesham (again by coach) for a further three days. During your stay in Stratford and Evesham we would organise various coach excursions (to Warwich castle, for example). For the last four days of your stay in England you would travel to London, staying in a hotel only 15 minutes by tube from the centre of the city.

The inclusive price per person for the two weeks (with half board in the hotels) would be £280. If you wish to fly (economy class) from Hannover to London, the cost would be £348 per person.If you wish to accept this offer, we would need to know exact numbers of participants by 4 June for an end of July departure.

Yours sincerely

F. Riley (Manager)

(Multilingual Business Handbook skeleton: K37, K74, K63, K77, K79, K51)

Continue the exchange of correspondence by composing a third letter (in German) on the basis of the following notes.

From: D. Hoeneß (Dürer-Gymnasium)

To: F. J. Riley

- We were interested to receive your proposed programme.

- We shall probably take up the offer (travelling by rail/coach).

- Is there any further discount for group size of 40?

- What is maximum and minimum group size for the programme you suggest?

- What deposit do you require on booking?

- What happens if 3 or 4 pupils have to cancel?

SECTION 11: PROPERTY: SALES AND RENTALS

This section is based on terms and expressions contained in Section L of the *MULTILINGUAL BUSINESS HANDBOOK*.

HOFFMANN UND KLINGER GmbH
HOCH- UND TIEFBAU

Kirchenstraße 45   2000 Hamburg 1

Telefon: 040 24 80 96
Telex: 2174324

Granger and Wilkes
Estate Agents
42 Littleton Mews
Fulham

London

England

Ihr Zeichen	Ihre Nachricht vom	Unser Zeichen WL/DK	Tag 4.6.19...

Betreff

Sehr geehrte Herren,

wir sind ein gut etabliertes Bauunternehmen mit Hauptsitz in Hamburg, und wir werden in 2 Monaten eine neue Zweigstelle in London eröffnen. Unser Chefingenieur Dr Martin Welser wird die Verwaltung dieser Zweigstelle übernehmen, und wir brauchen für ihn, ab 1. Oktober, eine Wohnung in London. Wir möchten die Wohnung für ungefähr 12 Monate mieten, und wir sind bereit, £900 pro Monat zu bezahlen.

Wir wären dankbar, wenn Sie uns sobald wie möglich mitteilen könnten, ob Sie zur Zeit eine geeignete Wohnung zur Verfügung haben. Wir sind auch ständig auf der Suche nach Unterkunft für unsere Lehrlinge während ihres Praktikums bei Firmen in Südengland. Es ist in den letzten Jahren ständig schwieriger geworden, geeignete preisgünstige Unterbringung für diese Leute zu finden. Wir wären Ihnen verbunden, wenn Sie uns in Verbindung mit einem Hotel oder einer Pension setzen könnten, die vielleicht in der Lage wäre, uns in dieser Angelegenheit zu helfen.

Mit freundlichen Grüßen

W. Linz
Personalleiter

(*Multilingual Business Handbook skeleton*: I1, J3, L12, L20)

Granger and Wilkes
Estates Agents/Valuers/Surveyors
42 Littleton Mews
Fulham
London
England

Tel: 01 436 3486
FAX: 01 328 9944

15.6.19...

Your Reference: WL/DK
Our Reference: MG/LD

Herrn
Wolfgang Linz
Hoffmann und Klinger GmbH
Kirchenstraße 45
2000 Hamburg 1
West Germany

Dear Mr Linz

Thank you for your letter of 4 June enquiring about the possibility of accommodation for your engineer, Dr Welser. We do not have many flats available at the moment at the price you mention, but there is one which may interest you, which we have just acquired. It is an apartment in a detached house in the suburbs, only 20 minutes by tube from the centre of town. It has a bedroom, living room, kitchen and bathroom, and is in a good neighbourhood. The rent is £800 per month, inclusive.

The owner wishes to let the apartment for one year whilst he is away in the United States. We need to know as soon as possible if you are interested. You could view the property next week if you are able to get to England then. Please let us know if you wish to do this.

With regard to your query about reasonably-priced accommodation for your apprentices, I suggest you contact Ms Rita Fulton, at the Student Accommodation Unit, Bailey College, Fulham Road, London. It is possible that she can suggest suitable short-term accommodation, particularly in the summer months. I hope this information is of help to you.

Yours sincerely

Martin Granger

Senior Partner

(*Multilingual Business Handbook skeleton:* L4, L7, L22, L11, L21)

Continue the exchange of correspondence by composing a third letter (in German) on the basis of the following notes.

From: W. Linz (Hoffmann und Klinger)

To: M. Granger (Granger and Wilkes)

• We are very interested in the apartment.

• We obviously need to see it before committing ourselves.

• Dr Welser himself can come to London next week.

• He will call in Wednesday p.m.

• Please arrange for him to see flat then.

• He will confirm then if he wishes to take it.

• We have contacted Ms Fulton by phone, and it appears that she can help out with accommodation problem.

DOMUS
Wohnungen und Appartements

Henningweg 36   7000 Stuttgart 1

Telefon: 0711 24 63 99
Telex: 722969

Childes and Harold
Estate Agents
27 Penfold Way

Canterbury

England

Ihr Zeichen	Ihre Nachricht vom	Unser Zeichen	Tag
		AF/DL	14.5.19...

Betreff
Ferienwohnungen im Schwarzwald

Sehr geehrte Herren,

wir haben mehrere Ferienwohnungen im Schwarzwald zu verkaufen oder zu vermieten, und ein Geschäftsfreund von Ihnen, Herr Peter Wayne, teilt uns mit, daß Sie vielleicht Kunden haben, die an diesen Wohnungen interessiert wären. Die Wohnungen befinden sich ausschließlich in kleinen geschmackvoll eingerichteten Neubauten etwa 9 Kilometer von Freudenstadt entfernt, und sie haben eine durchschnittliche Wohnfläche von 120 qm.

Die Miete für eine typische Wohnung (2 Schlafzimmer, Wohnzimmer, Küche, Badezimmer, Garage) beträgt DM900 in der Hochsaison, DM600 in der Vor- und Nachsaison.

Falls Sie Kunden haben, die an einem Kauf interessiert wären, liegen die Preise der Wohnungen zwischen DM360 000 und DM420 000. Wir könnten Darlehen durch unsere Versicherungsgesellschaft arrangieren. Im Juli bieten wir Ihnen einen kostenlosen Besichtigungsflug an. Wenn Sie daran Interesse haben, bitte setzen Sie sich mit uns in Verbindung.

Mit freundlichen Grüßen

Anton Forbach
Leiter

(*Multilingual Business Handbook skeleton:* L33, L11, L14, K67, K68, K69, L32, L34)

Childes and Harold

Estate Agents
27 Penfold Way
Canterbury
England

Tel: 0227 439246
Telex: HAR 634292

27.5.19...

Your Reference: AF/DL
Our Reference: AC/LD

Herrn
Anton Forbach
Domus
Henningweg 36
7000 Stuttgart 1
West Germany

Dear Mr Forbach

Thank you for your letter of 14 May. The information given to you by our mutual
acquaintance Peter Wayne is quite correct — we have several clients who have expressed
interest in holiday properties in Germany, particularly in the Black Forest and Bavaria. You
mention that loans can be arranged through your insurance company. In fact this is not a
problem, since we ourselves are able to arrange mortgages here for British clients.

I should be grateful if you could send me your brochure giving details of the flats so that we
may show it to potential purchasers. In your letter you quote typical monthly rents and
purchase prices. Could you let us know whether you can offer discounts for rental
agreements of longer than, say, 3 months?

We look forward to hearing from you again.

Yours sincerely

Antony Childes

Partner

(*Multilingual Business Handbook skeleton:* L32, L31, B12, L17)

Continue the exchange of correspondence by composing a third letter (in German) on the basis of the following notes.

From: Anton Forbach (Domus)

To: Antony Childes (Childes and Harold)

- We are pleased at expression of interest.

- Our brochure is not quite ready, as some flats were built very recently.

- Will send it a.s.a.p.

- We can offer discount of 15% for 'long' rentals (i.e. of 3 months or more).

- You do not mention if you are interested in an inspection flight — please confirm by telephone.

SECTION 12:   FINANCIAL REPORTS

This section is based on terms and expressions contained in Section B of the *MULTILINGUAL BUSINESS HANDBOOK*.

ANTON KARRER AG
Einbauküchen   Küchenmöbel   Kücheneinrichtungen
Hamburger Straße 48   6000 Frankfurt/Main

Telefon: 069 26 34 52
Telex: 412936

Mr L. Hutchins
Anton Karrer
36 Lenton Road

Warrington

England

Ihr Zeichen	Ihre Nachricht vom	Unser Zeichen	Tag
		TK/DN	14.6.19...

Betreff
Eventuelle Produktionseinstellung

Sehr geehrter Herr Hutchins,

unser Vorstand hat jetzt den Finanzbericht für das letzte Halbjahr veröffentlicht und, wie wir erwartet hatten, hat sich die Nachfrage nach bestimmten Artikeln abgeschwächt. Wie Sie bereits wissen, hatten wir dieses Problem schon besprochen. Wegen des allgemeinen Konjunkturabschwungs sind wir insbesondere auf dem englischen Markt auf Absatzschwierigkeiten gestoßen.

Vor zwei Tagen hat unser Vorsitzender Dr Gütemann eine außerordentliche Versammlung des Vorstands einberufen, um mögliche Lösungen zu diskutieren. Es wurde vorgeschlagen, daß die Anlage in Warrington die Herstellung von Kühlautomaten vor Ende des Jahres einstellen sollte, um sich ausschließlich auf die Produktion von Backöfen zu spezialisieren. Bevor wir aber zu einer endgültigen Entscheidung kommen, möchten wir die Sache mit Ihnen besprechen. Bitte teilen Sie mir sobald wie möglich mit, ob Sie in der Lage wären, in zwei Wochen nach Frankfurt zu fahren.

Ich sehe Ihrer baldigen Antwort gern entgegen.

Mit freundlichen Grüßen

Thomas Koch
Produktionsleiter

(*Multilingual Business Handbook skeleton:* M66, M64, M67, M5, J20, B2)

Anton Karrer
36 Lenton Road
Warrington
England

Tel: 0925 623487
FAX: 0925 554463

23.6.19...

Your Reference: TK/DN
Our Reference: LH/MP

Herrn
Thomas Koch
Anton Karrer AG
Hamburger Straße 48
6000 Frankfurt/Main
West Germany

Dear Mr Koch

Thank you for your letter of 14 June, which I received today. I have discussed with my colleague Mr Harris, the personnel manager, the possible consequences of the ceasing of production of certain items here at the Warrington plant. We believe it would mean that we should have to make about twenty workers redundant, and we obviously wish to avoid this.

I am very surprised to learn that there are problems with sales this year, as our turnover has increased by 6% in the last year, and, as you know, we have made considerable investment in the factory here.

I am able to come to Frankfurt at the end of next week, together with Mr Harris. We shall arrive on Friday afternoon, and I look forward to seeing you then and to having the opportunity of discussing this matter with you.

Yours sincerely

L. Hutchins

Production Manager

(*Multilingual Business Handbook skeleton:* J20, H19, M28, M32)

Continue the exchange of correspondence by composing a third letter (in German) on the basis of the following notes.

From: Thomas Koch (Anton Karrer AG)

To: L. Hutchins (Anton Karrer – GB)

- O.K. to come on Friday — we'll pick you up at airport. Please ring us with flight number

- Please try to assess more accurately the implications of reducing production

- Estimate of 20 job losses seems to us exaggerated

- Bring figures to meeting — Chairman wishes to see them (precise sales/production figures)

STIELICKE AG
Adenauerallee 96   4290 Bocholt

Telefon: 02871 4 15 63
Telex: 342946

J. Leeson plc
14 Rochester Way

Dover

England

Ihr Zeichen	Ihre Nachricht vom	Unser Zeichen	Tag
		RH/DM	15.9.19...

Betreff
Produktionssteigerung

Sehr geehrter Herr Leeson,

als unsere Tochtergesellschaft in Großbritannien wissen Sie, daß unsere Waren einen sehr guten Absatz in England gefunden haben. Unser Finanzbericht für das letzte Jahr zeigt, daß wir unseren Export um 15% erhöht haben, und daß unser Gesamtumsatz um 20% gestiegen ist.

Wir möchten diese günstige Marktposition festigen und ausbauen, aber wir haben dieses Jahr unsere vorhandenen Kapazitäten in der BRD voll ausgeschöpft. Wenn wir unseren Vorsprung behaupten wollen, brauchen wir neue Kapazitäten entweder in der BRD oder in Großbritannien. Ich weiß, daß der Finanzbericht für Ihre Firma erst Ende nächsten Monats veröffentlicht wird. Wir möchten aber wissen, wie es mit der Produktion in der Anlage in Dover steht. Wäre es z. B. möglich, einen Teil unserer Produktion vorläufig nach Dover zu verlegen?

Ihrer Stellungnahme sehe ich gern entgegen und verbleibe

mit freundlichen Grüßen

R. Haller
Leiter

(Multilingual Business Handbook skeleton: G38, M30, M28, M35, M36, M45, M46, J24)

J. Leeson plc
14 Rochester Way
Dover
England

Tel: 0304 349827
FAX: 0304 423366

23.9.19...

Your Reference: RH/DM
Our Reference: JL/NJ

Herrn
Richard Haller
Stielicke AG
Adenauerallee 96
4290 Bocholt
West Germany
Dear Mr Haller

Thank you for your letter of 15 September. I have discussed the matter you raised with our production manager, James Haughey. The report for the last year will apparently show that our production has also increased — by 7% in comparison with the previous year, largely because our sales were good in other countries.

However, we have not yet utilised to the full our existing capacity, and it is possible that we can help, particularly in the production of our joint 'Traveller' range of suitcases and bags.

We should need to know as soon as possible what amount of production you have in mind, as our short-term development programme includes one or two new ranges which would make full use of our current manufacturing capacity.

I hope this information is of use to you. Please contact me again if you require further details.

Yours sincerely

J. Leeson

(*Multilingual Business Handbook skeleton*: M22, M25, M26, M34, M45, M49, M50)

Continue the exchange of correspondence by composing a third letter (in German) on the basis of the following notes.

From: Richard Heller (Stielicke AG)

To: J. Leeson (Leeson plc)

- Thanks for the information you sent.

- It would help us greatly if you could take over some production of two ranges: 'Traveller' and 'Backpak'.

- Say 2,000 units per week of each.

- Forecasts show probably growth in total sales of 8% next spring.

- We don't want to lose this opportunity through lack of capacity.

- I shall fly over in about one week to discuss possibilities in more detail — please advise best arrival date.

SECTION 13: BANK AND POST OFFICE

This section is based on terms and expressions contained in Section O of the *MULTILINGUAL BUSINESS HANDBOOK*.

LANDESBANK – GIROZENTRALE
Kaiserstraße 96   6750 Kaiserslautern

Telefon: 0631 73666
Telex: 45683

Herrn
Roger Parsons
14 Clifton View

Romford

Essex

England

Ihr Zeichen	Ihre Nachricht vom	Unser Zeichen	Tag
		AM/DT	14.8.19...

Betreff

Sehr geehrter Herr Parsons,

für die Zeit Ihres Aufenthalts in Kaiserslautern (Februar bis Juli) hatten Sie ein Konto bei unserer Bank eröffnet – Kontonummer LD428357. Ich glaube, daß Ihr Praktikum in Kaiserslautern jetzt zu Ende ist. Sie haben aber noch nicht Ihr Konto aufgelöst. Das Konto steht jetzt in den roten Zahlen – es weist einen Minusbetrag von DM400 auf.

Ich muß Sie jetzt bitten, uns einen Scheck über DM400 zum Ausgleich dieses Minusbetrags zu schicken.

Mit freundlichen Grüßen

Anton Matthias
Leiter

(Multilingual Business Handbook skeleton: O5, O14, O18)

14 Clifton View
Romford
Essex
England

20.8.88

Herrn
Anton Matthias
Landesbank
Kaiserstraße 96
6750 Kaiserslautern
West Germany

Dear Mr Matthias

Thank you for your letter of 14 August. I was very surprised to hear that my account was in the red – I have certainly not made use of my cheque book since leaving Germany in July. I did however have a standing order to pay my monthly rent to the hostel I was in during my stay; the Novalis-Heim in Ofterdingenstraße. This was for DM 460 per month, which could explain the present problem. I can under the circumstances only assume that you have paid a month's rent for August after my departure, and I suggest you contact the Novalis-Heim to claim the money wrongly paid.

I wish to inform you also that I do not intend to close my account at the present time, as it is possible that I shall be in Germany again in the autumn.

Yours sincerely

Roger Parsons

(*Multilingual Business Handbook* skeleton: O18, O8, O9, O14)

Continue the exchange of correspondence by composing a third letter (in German) on the basis of the following notes.

From: Anton Matthias (Landesbank)

To: Roger Parsons

- We have re-checked our records — the amount you mention was paid to the hostel in August.

- It is, however, your responsibility to write to them, as your contract is with them.

- We still require payment of DM400 — within a week, or we must insist that you close your account with us forthwith.

- If not paid within one week, you will incur additional interest charges on the amount outstanding.

Theodor-Heuß-Straße 42
6300 Gießen

14.7.19...

Herrn
Dr A. Fields
Department of Languages
Mercia College of Advanced Technology

Birmingham

England

Sehr geehrter Herr Dr Fields,

mit neun anderen Studenten im Fachbereich Literatur- und Sprachwissenschaften an der
hiesigen Universität bin ich als eine der Studentinnen ausgewählt worden, die an dem
Austauschprogramm mit Ihrer Hochschule teilnehmen, und mein Professor Dr Udo Baertel
hat mir Ihren Namen als Kontaktperson gegeben. Ich möchte vor meiner Ankunft in
Birmingham einige Vorlesungen auswählen, die für mich geeignet wären. Ich studiere
Germanistik als Hauptfach mit Amerikanistik als Nebenfach, und ich interessiere mich
besonders für die amerikanische Literatur des neunzehnten Jahrhunderts. Ich wäre Ihnen
dankbar, wenn Sie mir ein Vorlesungsverzeichnis für das Wintersemester schicken könnten.

Hier in Gießen habe ich ein laufendes Konto bei der Landesbank, und meine Kollegen raten
mir, ein Konto bei einer Bank in Birmingham zu eröffnen. Ich möchte wissen, ob das
wirklich ratsam wäre, da ich nur 6 Monate in England bleibe. Wenn Sie der Meinung sind,
daß ich am besten ein Konto in England eröffne, wäre ich Ihnen verbunden, wenn Sie mir
eine Bank empfehlen und die nötigen Formulare zuschicken könnten.

Mit freundlichen Grüßen

Ute Kärntner

(Multilingual Business Handbook skeleton: O10, O5)

MERCIA COLLEGE OF ADVANCED TECHNOLOGY – BIRMINGHAM B23 4JS
Department of Applied Language Studies

Tel: 021 345 8735 ext.2367

Head of Department:
Dr T. Goode B.A. B. Litt. M.I.L.

25.7.88

Frl.
Ute Kärntner
Theodor-Heuß-Straße 42
6300 Gießen

Dear Ms Kärntner

Thank you for your letter of 14 July enquiring about our lecture courses, and about bank accounts here in England. With regard to the issue of bank accounts, there are various possibilities open to you: you could either open an account at a bank here in Birmingham (there are several suitable ones) and then transfer money from your existing account to your new one. Alternatively, you could of course bring travellers cheques with you, which can be cashed at most of the major banks here. The easiest method may be to get a Eurocheque card from your German bank, then you could simply cash cheques here without having to open a new account. Each method has its advantages and disadvantages. I have not sent you forms to fill in, as the formalities can be completed very quickly here.

I am afraid that I cannot send you a list of lectures, as we do not have such a publication in our institution. British colleges and universities differ from German ones in this respect. I suggest you discuss your particular needs and interests with one of my colleagues when you arrive.

I hope you will enjoy your stay in Birmingham, and I look forward to meeting you with the other exchange students at the beginning of term.

Yours sincerely

A. Fields
Lecturer in Hispanic Studies

(Multilingual Business Handbook skeleton: O5, O13, O22, O35)

Continue the exchange of correspondence by composing a third letter (in German) on the basis of the following notes.

From: U. Kärntner

To: A. Fields (Mercia C.A.T.)

- Thanks for your letter.

- Sorry to trouble you again, but could you check the following for me:

- How long to transfer money from my account to new one?

- What happens if I overdraw my English account?

- Is there any interest on current accounts in GB?

- If there is no full list of lectures, can you send me details of just one or two which may be relevant?

SECTION 14:   INSURANCE

This section is based on terms and expressions contained in Section P of the *MULTILINGUAL BUSINESS HANDBOOK*.

DIETRICH AG

Düsseldorfer Straße 96   4100 Duisburg

Telefon: 0203 35 67 48
Telex: 855669

Herrn
D. Jacobs
Atchison Fullerton plc
14 Wilton Way

Worcester

England

Ihr Zeichen	Ihre Nachricht vom	Unser Zeichen	Tag
		HM/DZ	3.5.19...

Betreff

Sehr geehrter Herr Jacobs,

wie Sie bereits wissen, werde ich in zwei Monaten meine neue Stelle in der Exportabteilung bei Ihrer Firma antreten. Ich werde zu der Zeit auch in meine neue Wohnung einziehen, und muß deshalb eine Sachversicherung abschließen. Da ich mein Auto mitbringe, und die Laufzeit meiner gegenwärtigen Autoversicherung im Juli zu Ende ist, brauche ich auch eine neue Autoversicherung.

Ich wäre Ihnen verbunden, wenn Sie mir einen zuverläßigen Versicherungsmakler empfehlen könnten. Ich könnte mich dann mit ihm in Verbindung setzen, bevor ich im Juli nach England fahre. Für Ihre baldige Antwort wäre ich dankbar.

Mit freundlichen Grüßen

Hans Müller

(Multilingual Business Handbook skeleton: P1, P3, P14, P34)

Atchison Fullerton plc
14 Wilton Way
Worcester

Tel: 0905 347527
Telex: AFUL42938

15.5.19...

Your Reference: HM/DZ
Our Reference: DJ/JL

Herrn
Hans Müller
Dietrich AG
Düsseldorfer Straße 96
4100 Duisburg
West Germany

Dear Herr Müller

Thank you very much for your recent letter. I am sorry I could not reply earlier, but I have been on a business trip to Switzerland, and I returned only yesterday.

I have for the last four or five years used a very reliable broker here in the town – P.J. Spreadbury and Partners, of 36 Kensington Parade. I am sure you will find them most helpful. If you can give me a few more details I can contact them for you and get some information on monthly premiums. Would you require comprehensive insurance for your car, for example, and what amount of property insurance do you require? If you let me have these details, I shall get in touch immediately with Spreadbury and Partners, so that you can take out the necessary insurance before you come to England.

Yours sincerely

D. Jacobs

(*Multilingual Business Handbook skeleton:* A48, A86, P34, P18, P26, P1)

Continue the exchange of correspondence by composing a third letter (in German) on the basis of the following notes.

From: Hans Müller (Dietrich AG)

To: D. Jacobs (Atchison Fullerton plc)

- Thanks for your helpful letter.

- I require fully comprehensive insurance, for a Volvo 740 — one year old.

- My age is 36.

- The amount of property insurance I require is £45,000.

- Could you also get details of a health insurance scheme for me?

ANTON PFAHLER VERSICHERUNG
Friedrichsallee 45   6800 Mannheim

Telefon: 0621 42 36 96
Telex: 463529

Ace Insurance Group
43 Donnington Avenue

Chesterfield

England

Ihr Zeichen	Ihre Nachricht vom	Unser Zeichen	Tag
		TM/DP	14.9.19...

Betreff

Sehr geehrte Herren,

am 9. August wurde das Auto von Herrn Dietrich Hennes in einem Zusammenstoß mit
einem Auto beschädigt, das von Herrn Peter Gray gefahren wurde. Herr Gray hatte zu der
Zeit keine Versicherungspapiere bei sich, hat aber Ihren Namen als Versicherungsgesellschaft gegeben. Die Police-Nummer sei, laut Herrn Gray, AN42 35/B42. Sein eigenes
Auto, das nur leicht beschädigt wurde, ist ein Renault 12 mit Kennzeichen BCP 669V.

In der Zwischenzeit hat Herr Hennes, dessen Auto durch unsere Firma versichert ist, sein
Auto reparieren lassen. Die Reparaturkosten betragen DM 1500, und wir müssen im Namen
unseres Kunden darauf bestehen, daß die Kosten von Ihrer Gesellschaft oder von Herrn Gray
zurückerstattet werden.

Wir sehen Ihrer baldigen Antwort gern entgegen.

Mit freundlichen Grüßen

Theodor Meiser
Autoversicherungsabteilung

(Multilingual Business Handbook skeleton: P12, G86)

Ace Insurance Group
43 Donnington Avenue
Chesterfield
England

Tel: 0246 324896
Telex: ACE 423764

22.9.19...

Your Reference: TM/DP
Our Reference: DGH/KW

Herrn
Theodor Meiser
Anton Pfahler Versicherung
Friedrichsallee 45
6800 Mannheim
West Germany
Dear Mr Meiser

We thank you for your letter of 14 September. We regret to inform you that we can be of little assistance in the affair you mention. Our policy-holder, Mr Gray, did not have a green card for his recent trip to Germany, despite our advice. This means that for the duration of his holiday he did not have comprehensive insurance cover. Apparently neither driver secured the names of witnesses of the incident, and this means that we cannot establish which driver was responsible for the accident. Under the circumstances, we regret that we are unable to accept your client's claim.

We can only suggest that you take up the matter yourself with Mr Gray, in the hope of obtaining reimbursement from him of the costs already incurred. We must add that we find it inadvisable for your client to have proceeded with repairs before clarifying the matter with the two insurance companies concerned.

Yours sincerely

D. Hopkins

Manager

_____

(*Multilingual Business Handbook skeleton*: P13, P28, P26, P30, F83, P20)

Continue the exchange of correspondence by composing a third letter (in German) on the basis of the following notes.

From: Theodor Meiser (Pfahler Versicherung)

To: D. Hopkins (Ace Insurance)

- Our client did furnish the names of three witnesses – your information regarding this aspect is incorrect.

- All three witnesses claim that Mr Gray was responsible.

- We are forwarding copies of their reports to you.

- Even without a green card, Mr Gray must have had 3rd party insurance.

- This covers him for damage to our client's car.

- We must insist again on full reimbursement.

SECTION 15: OFFICE TERMINOLOGY AND TECHNOLOGY

This section is based on terms and expressions contained in Section Q of the *MULTILINGUAL BUSINESS HANDBOOK*.

INFOTEK GmbH
Schottenstraße 48   7032 Sindelfingen

Telefon: 07031 9 3063
Telex: 7265899

Herrn
Michael Hales
Richards Pearce plc
72 Willingham Avenue

Coventry

England

Ihr Zeichen	Ihre Nachricht vom	Unser Zeichen	Tag
		AS/DL	9.3.19..

Betreff

Sehr geehrter Herr Hales,

von meinem Bekannten Norbert Ullstein habe ich erfahren, daß Sie für Ihr Büro einen Computer brauchen, um Ihre elektrischen Schreibmaschinen zu ersetzen. Ich glaube, daß unser neues Modell, das NDL 428, Ihren Bedürfnissen entsprechen würde. Dieser neue Personalcomputer hat einen hochauflösenden Bildschirm, einen 512KB Hauptspeicher, eine eingebaute 10MB Festplatte und einen Drucker mit verschiedenen Einstellmöglichkeiten. Mit dieser Maschine erhalten Sie kostenlos unser Textverarbeitungsprogramm, das auch für 'Anfänger' besonders bedienungsfreundlich ist. An unser Modell NDL 428B kann ein Modem angeschlossen werden, das Ihnen die Verbindung mit verschiedenen Informationssystemen ermöglicht.

Weil die Maschine völlig IBM-kompatibel ist, ist die Bedienung von vielen Software-Paketen möglich. Mit dem neu entwickelten Betriebssystem können Sie Texte bis zur maximalen Größe der Diskettenkapazität bearbeiten. Wir sind überzeugt, daß dieses neue Modell Ihnen zu einem sehr günstigen Preis Leistungsfähigkeit und Vielseitigkeit bietet.

Wenn Sie weitere Informationen erhalten möchten, bitte setzen Sie sich mit mir in Verbindung.

Mit freundlichen Grüßen

Anton Schöpp
Verkaufsleiter

(*Multilingual Business Handbook skeleton:* A30, C3, Q8, Q29, Q9, Q63)

RICHARDS PEARCE PLC
72 Willingham Avenue   Coventry

Tel: 0203 538463
FAX: 0203 727272

18.3.19..

Your Reference: AS/DL
Our Reference: MH/BS

Herrn
Anton Schöpp
Infotek GmbH
7032 Sindelfingen
West Germany
Dear Mr Schöpp

Thank you for your letter of 9 March. Herr Ullstein is correct in informing you that we are looking for a computer to replace our existing equipment in our office here in Coventry. We need the new machines by the end of May. In addition to word processing software we shall also need a database capable of storing details of our 2000 employees.

I should be interested to hear what peripherals (laser printer, modem etc.) you could supply, and at what cost. We have recently received an offer from another firm to supply a complete system of two workstations with all software for £6,500. They are also offering a low-cost maintenance contract for the second and subsequent years, in addition to their one-year guarantee.

If you wish to discuss our requirements further before we commit ourselves, we should be pleased to hear from you again.

Yours sincerely

Michael Hales

Office Manager

(*Multilingual Business Handbook skeleton:* Q9, Q70, Q105, Q115, Q36, Q142, Q125, C23)

Continue the exchange of correspondence by composing a third letter (in German) on the basis of the following notes.

From: Anton Schöpp (Infotek)

To: Michael Hales (Richards Pearce plc)

- We could supply the required machines by the end of May — no problem.

- Our deal could include a database at very low cost.

- We can supply any peripherals you require — a price list is included.

- The price quoted by the other company seems to us rather low if they are including a good-quality printer and software. We advise you to be cautious.

- We should be pleased to discuss your particular requirements in detail — would next week be convenient? Our rep is in your area then.

MASCHINENBAU LDT
Förstenstraße 43   3300 Braunschweig

Telefon: 0298 43 68 29
Telex: 952648

Herrn
Martin Dryden
Compusis
42 Weatherall Avenue

Reading

England

Ihr Zeichen	Ihre Nachricht vom	Unser Zeichen	Tag
		LD/MF	14.7.19..

Betreff
Installation von Arbeitsplatzcomputern

Sehr geehrter Herr Dryden,

wie Sie nach Ihrem Gespräch mit unserem Direktor Herrn Lattek bereits wissen, haben wir
vor, unsere Büroarbeit in der Niederlassung in Norwich weitgehend zu rationalisieren, und
zwar auf der Basis der neuen Niederlassung in Münster. Die genauen Einzelheiten kann ich
mit Ihnen besprechen, wenn Sie im nächsten Monat nach Braunschweig fahren. Was die
Hardware betrifft, brauchen wir 4 komplett ausgestattete Arbeitsplatzcomputer, jeder mit
Hauptspeicher mit mindestens 512KB, und mit eingebauter Festplatte (15MB). Jede
Maschine soll ein 3.5" Laufwerk mit mindestens 300KB Speicherkapazität (unformatiert)
pro Seite haben. Wir brauchen auch einen Matrix-Drucker, der in Korrespondenzqualität mit
ca. 35 Zeichen pro Sekunde drucken kann, und einen Laserdrucker. Das ganze System muß
selbstverständlich IBM-kompatibel sein. Unser Telex im Büro soll durch eine Fax-Maschine
ersetzt werden – für Ihre weiteren Vorschläge wäre ich dankbar.

Neben einem Textverarbeitungsprogramm brauchen wir ein zuverläßiges und
leistungsfähiges Datenbanksystem. Ich weiß, daß es zur Zeit eine verwirrende Anzahl von
verschiedenen Programmen und Paketen auf dem Markt gibt – eine endgültige Entscheidung
kann nur nach unseren weiteren Gesprächen getroffen werden. Die Kosten von Hardware,
Software und Installation müssen bis Ende August veranschlagt werden, damit sie vom
Vorstand im September genehmigt werden können.

Mit freundlichen Grüßen

Lothar Delmenhorst

(*Multilingual Business Handbook skeleton:* Q67, Q68, Q113, Q122, Q115, Q41, Q70, Q53)

COMPUSIS
Business Information Systems Consultants
42 Weatherall Avenue   Reading

Tel: 0734 427384
FAX: 0734 221188

22.7.19..

Your Reference: LD/MF
Our Reference: MD/HS

Dear Mr Delmenhorst

Thank you for your letter regarding the proposed installation of our new electronic office equipment in your Norwich branch. As you are already aware, we shall be pleased to undertake the installation work for you, and to advise you on the machines and software which are best suited to your needs.

We have recently been recommending a computer which is new on the market, a very high quality machine at a competitive price – the Fernhart 'Personal', which meets all your technical requirements. This computer retails at a price 20% lower than that of many other competing models, and has a two-year guarantee. A software package is included in the price: a word-processing system and a spreadsheet. A database is available at extra cost from Fernhart, but we ourselves would recommend purchase of a system we have supplied to many customers, and which has proved most efficient.

We would estimate the cost of the whole system – 4 workstations, 2 printers, and the appropriate software, to be in the region of £15,000. If you have any further queries, please contact me again. I shall of course be coming over to see you shortly.

Yours sincerely

M. Dryden

Installations Manager

(*Multilingual Business Handbook skeleton:* Q70, Q102, Q101, Q71, Q56, Q142)

Continue the exchange of correspondence by composing a third letter (in German) on the basis of the following notes.

From: L. Delmenhorst (Maschinenbau LDT)

To: M. Dryden (Compusis)

- Thanks for your very informative letter.

- I'd like to clarify a couple of points:

- You don't mention the FAX machine in your letter — is this included in the quoted price?

- Is the installation cost included?

- How long would installation take, and what training would you offer to our personnel? Bear in mind that several of them have never used a word processor before.

- Could you also send us a quotation which itemises the individual pieces of equipment?

LinguaWrite

Automatic multilingual business letters

What is LinguaWrite?

LinguaWrite is an exciting and versatile software package for creating business letters in the *five* major European languages. LinguaWrite is the ideal software companion for the *Multilingual Business Handbook* and *Multilingual Business Correspondence Course*. It is specially developed for use in business and education.

What can I do with LinguaWrite?

Using LinguaWrite you can:

* have access to the *Multilingual Business Handbook* database of 2000 specialised phrases in each language: English, French, German, Italian and Spanish
* put these phrases into your word-processor without needing to type them
* search the complete database for key words or multiple key words or limit this search to a particular section
* browse through the database, as if leafing through the book, and select the required phrase at the press of a key
* enter the alphanumeric code given in the book and have the translation instantly
* with just a few keystrokes, build up business letters, like building blocks, instantly on screen
* change the source and target languages at will
* change the menus and messages into any of the five languages at a touch of a key.

The program caters for accents and special non-English characters and these appear correctly in your word-processor as long as it can support the full character set. (An additional package is available to customise national keyboards that do not support the full range of European characters.)

Simple to use

The program is very simple to operate and you can begin work in a few minutes. The accompanying manual is clear and straightforward and written for those who are unfamiliar with computer technology as well as for more expert users.

LinguaWrite is available for BBC and IBM (and compatible) computers.

For more information and prices, please contact:

MultiLingua
FREEPOST
LONDON W4 3BR
Tel.: 01–995–0478